KOHILA

THE SHAPING
OF AN
INDIAN NURSE

BY

AMY CARMICHAEL

He took me from a fearful pit,
And from the miry clay,
And on a rock He set my feet,
Establishing my way.

He put a new song in my mouth,
Our God to magnify:
Many shall see it, and shall fear,
And on the Lord rely.

- *Ps.40, Scottish Metrical Version.*

DOHNAVUR FELLOWSHIP PUBLICATIONS INDIA

ISBN 81-901277-0-5

First Published   1939
Second Published   1947
Third Published   1956
Fourth Published   2001

Published by :

The Dohnavur Fellowship
Dohnavur - 627 102
Tirunelveli Dist. T.N.
S. India

Printed by :

Alleluia Print Services
Madurai -625 006, India.

APS / 5T / 02 / 2001

Front Cover Photo :
The girl KOHILA with a baby in the center.

FOREWORD

WHEN the happy possessor of one of the copies printed of *Edward Grey and his Birds* turned to the end of the book and found fifteen photographs set one after the other, he had, I expect, the pleasant feeling that a child has when it is given the unexpected to enjoy. I hope that something of this feeling will be with those who buy this book. It is the story of the shaping of a little Indian girl for soldiership on spiritual battlefields. But so many have asked for pictures of the everyday life among our children that when a guest was with us who had time to sit down among them and make friends, and to "take" them just as they are, we were very glad to be able at last to give what had been wanted.*

"Be the first, wherever there is a sacrifice to be made, a self-denial to be practised, or an impetus to be given"- the pictures touch that part of the training. They are vital to the story.

No work that is set on following the Crucified escapes the Cross. It would not wish to do so. Sooner or later, if those who must give account of it to God do not weaken on some point of loyalty to Truth, they will find themselves bearing the Reproach of Christ.

Little is said of this in Kohila's story, but the fact that it is so gives depth to the book, just as it gives depth to all the most vital books that have ever been written. And the reader whose days have not been passed in the pleasant shallows of life recognises something in a sentence here and there which the heart understands without explanation. Deep calleth unto deep.

---

* Please refer to the note inserted immediately before the photographs

FOREWORD - Contd. 2

The story is about a girl, and so, naturally there is more about girls than about boys in these pages. But our boys are brought up on the same lines of soldiership. For them also we covet the spirit that "neither fears nor flatters any flesh," and makes a "conscience of speaking of truth when none knoweth but God," and lives to love and serve, without thought of earth's poor dusty gains. So some of the later chapters which tell us about a company of girls whom Kohila joined, might equally have been about His young Knights and the self-discipline asked of them.

After all, boy or girl, man or woman, makes no difference. We are all called to Knighthood. " O God, my heart is fixed, my heart is fixed; I will sing and give praise" is a great word for these changeful days. God give it to us to belong to the Order of the Fixed Heart.

Though sun and moon and stars be not, the heavens a vanished scroll,
The pillars of the earth are His. Be fixed in God, my soul.
The waves may roar, the nations rage, and yet at His command
At the four corners of the earth the four great angels stand,
And swiftly hasteneth the day foretold in His sure word:
The kingdoms of the earth shall be the kingdoms of the Lord.

A.C.
Dohnavur Fellowship
Dohnavur, S.India

THE DOHNAVUR FELLOWSHIP

THE work known by this name began in 1901. There exists in connection with the temples of India a system like that which obtained in such places as the great temple of Corinth with its Thousand Servants. Young children trained for temple service have no chance to grow up good. They are the most defenceless of God's innocent creatures. We gave ourselves to save them, and as we lived in a village called Dohnavur the work became known by that name.

The story of the Fellowship is told in *Gold Cord*. It has now been made illegal to dedicate a young child to a god. But as all who know the East know, there are ways by which a law can be evaded. Apart from that, there are very many children in danger of being brought up for wrong purposes. So the need for the work continues whatever the law may be.

In 1918 we began to take boys too, for they also are used in the temples, and still more often in the evil dramatic societies and cinemas of Southern India.

The work is difficult and asks for all that we have to give. There are griefs, but there are far more joys. The greater number of the first generation of children are spending their lives in the service of their Saviour, and for the blessing of their country.

From the first we thought of the children as our own. We did not make a Home for them, when they came to us they were at home. And so from the beginning we were a family, never an institution; and we all, Indian and European, men and women, live and work together on the lines of an Indian family, each contributing what each has to offer for the help of all. We have no salaried workers, Indian or foreign; make no appeal for funds; and authorize none to be made for us. We have never lacked; as the needs grew supplies came; and as we advance we find that our Unseen Leader is moving on before us. There are over eight hundred in the family. We have village work and medical work.

We have no workers who are only preachers. "We have heard the preaching, *can you show us the life of your Lord Jesus?*" said a Hindu to one of us. Our Master who not only preached and taught, but went about *doing* good, and His servant, St. Paul, who not only taught publicly and from house to house, but laboured, working with his own hands, gave us the pattern that we as a Fellowship were intended to follow. So the evangelist shares in the practical work of life—doctoring, nursing, teaching, building, engineering, farming, and so on.

We come from various parts of the household of God; but we never find this to be any hindrance to harmony, for we meet at the centre, above and below difference. And to be one in love to our Lord and in faith in the Book, the sum of whose words is truth, makes for vital unity.

A.C.

NOTE

Accãl	-	older sister.
Ammã	-	as used here, mother.
		(The word has other friendly uses)
Annãchie	-	older brother, protector, a chivalrous word.
Sittie	-	mother's younger sister.

N.B. - In Kohila, "Ko" rhymes with "No".

Dohnavur songs and rhymes are in *Italics*.

We have left Amma's original note 'THE DOHNAVUR FELLOWSHIP' preferring to clarify one or two points rather than rewrite it :

♦ Some of our children are saved from moral danger, but the majority are saved from infanticide.

♦ Our boy's work came to an end in 1984 and since then only girl babies and small children have joined our Family which, all together, numbers over 440.

♦ The buildings the boys occupied are now put to full use. In 1981 the Fellowship formed the Santhosha Educational Society to administer a co-educational, English-medium boarding-school for the children of missionaries of Indian nationality, working all over India. There are over 500 students studying in Stds. I-XII.

- Many of those in succeeding generations are also serving their Saviour in numerous ways in the towns and villages of India, as well as here at home.

- We no longer have any permanent workers from overseas nor residential village work.

- We do now have two Indian doctors and three dentists serving in our hospital, who are salaried workers.

INDEX TO FIRST LINES

OF DOHNAVUR FELLOWSHIP SONGS

CONTENTS

PART 1. CHILDHOOD

PART 2. GIRLHOOD

CONTENTS - Contd. 2

PART 3. SOLDIERSHIP

To

All who understand

To

All who understand

PART 1

CHILDHOOD

IN *Centuries of Meditations*, edited by Bertram Dobell, Traherne tells of how the first light which shined in his Infancy in its primitive and innocent clarity was totally eclipsed, insomuch that he was fain to learn it all again. "If you ask me how it was eclipsed? Truly by the customs and manners of men, which, like contrary winds, blew it out by an innumerable company of other objects, rude, vulgar, and worthless things, that like so many loads of earth and dung did overwhelm and bury it.... All men's thoughts and words were about other matters. They all prized new things which I did not dream of. And finding no one syllable in any man's mouth of those things, by degrees they vanished, my thoughts (as indeed what is more fleeting than a thought?) were blotted out; and at last ill the celestial, great, and stable treasures to which I was born, as wholly forgotten, as if they had never been.... By this let nurses, and those parents that desire Holy Children, learn to make them possessors of Heaven and Earth betimes; to remove silly objects from before them, to magnify nothing but what is great indeed, and to talk of God to them, and of His works and ways before they can either speak or go."

1. KOHILA

I see some sparkles...
Which elder days may happily bring forth.
Richard II.

Children are born persons.
Ourselves, C. M. Mason.

SHE was about four years old, and she arrived, as many another child has after a long journey, tired, dishevelled, frightened and shy. Her bright dark eyes looked up at us out of a tangle of rough curls. She was rather like a small brown Skye terrier, but Kohila was her name, and it means Cuckoo. Presently, reassured, she curled up on a friendly knee like a kitten who wants to be petted. Then she was fed and bathed and put on a mat with a shawl over her (for it was our chilly December) to sleep off her tiredness. And though, because she had gone through strange and hardening experiences, she was wary, and did not at once make friends, unhappy things were soon forgotten, and she slipped into her place as if it had been created for her—which, of course, it had. It is difficult to gather anything of interest about those months: they were just happy.

The first great outstanding joy which was all her own was the celebration of her Coming-day in the following December. For as we do not often know birthdays, we keep, instead, the anniversary of the day a child comes to us. Then, if he be a boy, he is dressed in a tiny grown-up *vèshti*, and feels a man; if a girl, the easy, straight-up-and-down *camasu* is exchanged for a *sāri*, the perfect garment of India's women. There is nothing daintier than a little girl in a *sāri*, but it is very hard to keep tidy, and tidiness was not Kohila's strong point. But who minds anything on a Coming-day? Special flowers are in her room that day, and with flowers tucked into her curls,

3

and her small face beaming, she comes for her presents; first, a morsel of soap which is never confused with nursery soap, but her very own; the second, any other delight we have to give. And then (no child will ever willingly miss this) there is a minute's prayer alone. It is not hard to lead a child to the Lover of children. I do not think Kohila ever remembered when she first began to love Him who loved her so much, though a day was to come later when she recognised Him as the Lord and Master of her life.

These little things do not sound very important, but they help to make home. The bird, who is free to fly all over the place, is persuaded to stay in his night-cage for a while on his Day, and the cage is decorated and carried to the House of Prayer. The swing is garlanded. Nothing is too small to have a Coming-day.

For nothing is too small to help towards the building up of something like that which an old writer describes after quoting the words, "The Wolf shall dwell with the Lamb, and the Leopard shall lye down with the Kid." 'See here a Kingdom of God on the Earth; it is nothing else but a Kingdom of mere Love, where all HURT and DESTROYING is done away, and every Work of Enmity changed into one united Power of Heavenly Love.—But observe again and again, whence this comes to pass, that God's Kingdom on Earth is, and can be nothing else, but the Power of reigning Love."*

There are times when the Power of reigning Love seems remote from this land, and any attempt to create a little place where that Power may reign is keenly contested.

But I do not think this can possibly be understood except by one who has lived for many years, not merely in India, but on the floor of India.

---

* *An humble, earnest, and Affectionate Address to the Clergy.*
By William Law. Printed in Paternoster Row, London. 1761.

For India is like a wide reach of water on whose surface many beautiful reflections may be seen. But go deeper, and you find slime. Many feel it unseemly even to allude to the crawling life below. It is true that the history of every nation is full of stained pages. The historian is not expected to palliate them. But where India is concerned it is different. If you must use that sincere thing, salt, be careful to sugar your salt. Avoid above all things unsugared salt, for it is most offensive. Be like him of whom it is written, he shall come in peaceably and obtain the kingdom by flatteries.

But sugar stings no conscience, attracts no warrior, wins no vital prayer. India has lost help in her need because of this sugary writing. The valiant go elsewhere. And yet there is no sterner field and none more sorrow-filled, and surely none dearer to the heart of God. And to those who love her, there is none dearer on earth.

The purpose of this story, however, is not to tell of grievous things, but of the happiest of happy things, the spiritual training of a child for soldiership.

So we leave unwritten much that could be written about what underlies all that we are trying to do. And words which we often sing shall tell our prayer for ourselves and for our comrades who are called to fight the fight, and run the race, not among the shadows—though those shadows cannot be forgotten—but in the light of God. *The heart that seeks His pleasure shall rejoice* is the Septuagint rendering of I Chron. 16: 10. Ministers who do His pleasure, is one of His kind names for us. Well may we rejoice.

This is the prayer:

> *Let them that love Thee be as the sun*
> *When he goeth forth in his might,*
> *Till the stars of evening kindle one by one,*
> *So let them run in light.*

Let them that love Thee, breathing heavenly air,
And refreshed in peace, be strong,
Till the bells of evening, joyful and aware,
Call them to evensong.

2. THE UPPER SPRINGS, AND THE NETHER SPRINGS

And it came to pass, as she came unto him, that she moved him to ask of her father a field: and she lighted off her ass; and Caleb said unto her, What wouldest thou? Who answered, Give me a blessing; for thou hast given me a south land; give me also springs of water. And he gave her the upper springs, and the nether springs.

About pruning: a Quaker lady of olden time had a concern to visit American Friends. On the first night after her arrival in the States, she dreamed that she was walking in her host's orchard, pruning his fruit-trees. Presently the owner of the orchard appeared and said quietly, *"Friend, I'll thank thee to let me prune my own fruit-trees."*

Those were grown-up trees, of course; the story chastens any undue tendency to prune such. But even with little trees it is good to remember that we are only under-gardeners.

WHEN, some years before Kohila came, a Greater than Caleb had asked a lesser one than his daughter, What wouldest thou for these children? she had answered Him:

Make them good soldiers of Jesus Christ: let them never turn themselves back in the day of battle.

Let them be winners and helpers of souls.

Let them live not to be ministered unto, but to minister.

Make them loyal; let them set loyalty high above all things.

Make them doers, not mere talkers; make them sound.

Let them enjoy hard work and choose hard things rather than easy. Forbid that they be slackers. Make them trustworthy. Give them grit.

Make them wise, for it is written, He hath no pleasure in fools.

Let them pass from dependence on us to dependence on Thee.

Let them never come under the dominion of earthly things; keep them free.

Let them grow up healthy, happy, friendly and keen to make others happy.

Give them eyes to see the beauty of the world and hearts to worship its Creator. Cause them to be quick to recognise "the figures of the true."

Let them be gentle to beast and bird; let cruelty be hateful to them.

May they walk, O Lord, in the light of Thy countenance.

Let this be the inheritance of these children—the upper springs and the nether springs of life.

And for ourselves we asked that we might learn how to brace and never weaken. "God is my strong salvation," we asked that we might train them to say that word and live that life, and pour themselves out for others unhindered by self.

So with these thoughts clear in view, there was no softness, though there was much tenderness, in the nurseries. From the beginning work was mixed with play. There were pots and pans to scrub and brass vessels to polish, and the ground round the nurseries to be swept with brooms made of grasses fastened together in an ingenious Indian way; and there were floors to wash. These floors are of tiles, which are made locally, and are dull and uninteresting when they arrive. But we soon change that. Continual scrubbing with old rags gives them a shine which reflects almost like red water. Later on, the Annãchies followed the same tradition which cuts across the softening Indian way of bringing up boys. And from nursery days onward one of the most vigorously-sung songs always has been, "Hate not laborious work" (a line straight from Ecclesiasticus), "joy, joy, is in it."

But one day somebody asked for a Scrubbing-song, which a boy or girl, who was not keen on laborious work, might sing if so inclined. Before long a small person was heard singing,

I scrub my pots, I scrub my pans,
I scrub my brasses and my cans,
I sweep and scrub each red floor-tile
Till I can see it smile.

And as I scrub I feel so gay
It might be my own Coming-day;
For work is such a jolly thing
It makes one want to sing.

When I was very young, my old nurse in all innocence taught me a rhyme which would have horrified my Puritan parents. The first verse runs,

Matthew, Mark, Luke and John
Bless the bed that I lie on.
Four angels to my bed,
Two at the bottom, two to head,
Two to hear me when I pray,
Two to bear my soul away.

We did not teach our children that rhyme or anything like it, but we did teach them more than children are usually taught about the angels, for we think of them as friends. Kohila and her little sisters therefore learned to keep the backs of their nurseries as tidy as the fronts, so that the angels (and above all the Lord of the angels) might see nothing displeasing anywhere. Long afterwards, when Kohila was head girl of a nursery, someone said of her, "She finds it hard to be tidy, for her hair is the sort of hair that never looks tidy; but she is always very particular about the backs of places." Perhaps no word could have more refreshingly reminded me of those early days when one of us used to take a little curly-headed Kohila round to the back of her nursery, and pointing to some evident carelessness say, "If the angels came here, what would they say about *that*?"

3. REMOVE SILLY OBJECTS

I want to climb the air,
I want to find the stair,
But I cannot find it anywhere.

I know quite well there are
Great things up there—far, far;
I should like to stand upon a star.

But though I cannot go
So far away; quite low,
Many little, lovely, dear things grow.

ALMOST at once, one of our thoughts about the upper and the nether springs was unintentionally assailed, for friends, in the kindness of their hearts, sent us toys and picture-books of a sort that perplex and pervert the eyes of children.

I think that even in this age of the cult of the hideous (in certain directions at least), some feel the same; and such will understand why we tried to make the beautiful that they could see, and the still more beautiful which is just out of sight, mean much to our children.

Sometimes, before they had learned "to go" in the common paths of life, the Unseen drew them so that they wanted to see it at once, and one day two adventurous friends of Kohila's trotted demurely down the drive and turned out of the gate into the village street. They met a carter, a friend of the family, and said firmly, "Do us the favour to drive us at once to heaven. Drive us there, O elder brother; we wish to see the Place."

Can any child whose parents cared for such things forget the joy of her first pocket-lens, and later her microscope? We wanted to fill our children's minds with happy memories like those that filled ours. And from little down to least, with hardly an exception, they responded. Often we came upon one or another of them silently and quite alone gazing at the gold of dawn, or the rose of sunset, or at light on water, or at some new flower or blossoming tree.

A baptism evening by the water-side was one of our greatest opportunities, though, of course, every day had its opportunities. But on those evenings, instead of hastening home after the Service, we used to sit quietly in long lines on the bank, and watch the changing colours of the sunset, and the birds flying across the water, till the still beauty had time to sink into our being and become part of us. Then, with crimson lanterns carried by the older children, we streamed homewards across the Plain. I do not say that we always succeeded in everything (life is made of endeavours, not of achievements); but we had this great help: the Indian eye is quick to recognise fine gold, if only it be not dazzled by tinsel.

Garlands made of beheaded flowers we could not banish; they are part of Indian life; and, after all, we of the West have our daisy-chains and cowslip-balls. But we avoided the garish, and encouraged the Japanese custom of setting each flower apart as nearly as possible as she grows, so that she might show her beauty in her own way.

Another great help was ours. The lot has fallen unto us in a fair ground, especially after the Rains have filled the long reaches of water that lie under the hills. "How temptingly the landscape shines. The air breathes invitation" after rain. At other seasons the water disappears, the reddish colour of the earth is relieved only by the various trees which never wholly undress, and in some places by palms. But there are always the mountains; and except when two monsoons fail in succession, our garden world is green. But beauty does not make goodness, though one often fancies it should, and many a time when a new, pretty little room was built, one found oneself repeating two lines from *Brand*,

> Could but the new-built house impart
> Clean spirit and regenerate heart!

"I should like to adopt a baby," said someone about the time we began to adopt, "but if I did I should shut her up in a drawer as soon as she began to have a little soul." And we understood. There is something terrible in the thought of the two babies painted by Francois Drouais in the picture which has lately been discovered, growing up to be what those babies became. Why did they not—those two innocents with their little round faces and wondering eyes—fly to heaven in their innocence? Why did they live to become the fatuous Louis XVI and the infamous Regent?

It is a solemn thing, however one regards it, to have to do with the moulding of a child—that wax which so quickly becomes marble, as someone has said. Nothing is unimportant in the trifles of nursery life, and nothing is so rewarding as the nurture of little children.

It was not easy to do what we wanted to do, even in the simple matter of teaching them to distinguish good from bad in what they saw. Civilisation, so called, has muddied the Eastern taste, which, taking it all round, is a far finer thing than the Western type as commonly imported. For just as some Eastern nations export things that they would never use themselves, so do we of the West export rubbish to the East; and very often the children saw the opposite of all that we had taught them to care for, made much of and admired. (It is a curious fact that the kitchen in a well-to-do Eastern house is sometimes the only room in the house where one can be without seeing some Western vulgarity. The kitchen keeps to its old ways, and its beautiful earthen or brass or copper vessels are still its unconscious adornments, unless the cheap and nasty have invaded it in the shape of enamel and other ugly ware.) Except for this counter-influence, we found no difficulty in leading our little ones into the paths that we ourselves had found so pleasant.

Before Kohila had been long with us, the stuff she was made of was tested. She began to limp. She had the happy knack of taking things by the right handle, so she made no fuss, but the lameness increased.

Some years earlier we had been given that longed-for benediction, a Sittie, Mabel Wade, who was a trained nurse. When she came to us in 1907 she had printed on a card in her room words that we always associate with her, *A little thing is a little thing; but faithfulness in little things is a very great thing.* India is rich in love-names; she was the first of twelve whose names mean Very dear, Beloved. If she had been here she would have undertaken Kohila, but she was on furlough then. So Kohila had to be sent to hospital, and alone; for we had no one whom we could spare to be with her. Poor little Kohila was brave, and the medicals, according to the blessed custom of medicals, were very good to her. She was contented and gave no one any trouble; but it was a relief to have her home well.

We happened to be at the sea when she was ready to return, and Arul Dasan, the only son of the family at that time, went for her. One of her friends who was about the same age remembers how she arrived, rather shy again and curled-up in the old kitten-way, and how she gazed in astonishment at the tragedy which at that moment chanced to be enacted. For the children had discovered a great pailful of delicious boiled gram (pulse given to horses here), and thinking, in their greedy young hearts, that it was far too good for a horse, they set to and ate it all. The horse-keeper appeared soon afterwards, and naturally he was as indignant as the mother of those children was ashamed. "So you told us to stand in a row, and you gave us each one a slap on our hands with the horse's strap, and you made us apologise to the horse-keeper" (I hope they apologised to the horse), "and then you gave him money to buy more gram; and Kohila looked on solemnly and never spoke a word."

It does not sound a nice home-coming, but, after all, there is something for most of us in the story of John Brown's frankness when Queen Victoria had been severe with a young footman "for dropping a silver salver with a clatter in her presence." Said John Brown, "What are ye daein' tae that puir laddie? Have ye never drappit onything yersel?" (What a queen she must have been to possess and to value such a servant!)

So we forgave and forgot, and were soon in the midst of the riotous joys of the sea, where, holding hands, we bathed in the edge of the surf. We used to count the little dancing things when we had them safely out, for the waves were enormous, and could easily have swept us off to the Pole, our nearest land as we stand at the end of India.

4. THE CUTTLE-FISH'S INK-POT

"Croak, croak, croak!
Do you like your folk?"
"Yes!" says the little Jackdaw.

T.E.Brown.

"THE fishermen gave us three baby cuttle-fishes. One was dead, so we opened it" (ghastly children), "and found the cuttle-fish's ink-pot inside it; and we mixed the ink with water, and the letter we wrote to you was written with that ink"—thus one of Kohila's friends in a later year. And I felt as I read the letter written with ink from the cuttle-fish's ink-pot how much I should like to dip my pen in a pot of golden ink as I write of those happy yesterdays.

It is good to think that many ink-pots of golden ink would be needed if any one attempted to tell in full the story of our to-days. There were happy days in the past. There are happy days about us now. Blessed be happiness—the bubbling-over happiness of little children. It must seem a piteous thing to the people in the Celestial Country, that so many make themselves and others unhappy in so beautiful a world. And we share their grief, if one may speak of angels grieving.

Some years before Kohila came to us, we began to have a day of Prayer once a month for children in danger, and part of the time was given to what a friend called our litany. Each child old enough to do so named a town, and as each town was named, all united in the petition, "Gracious Lord, we pray Thee to save the children there." From hundreds of these towns and cities children have been saved, and in many cases, especially at the beginning, there was a long battle fought before the child was saved. But I think we who are called to such battles have much to learn from Earl Haig. It is written that when victory was granted there was no trite moralising, no paean of triumph. "What he had further to say upon the subject was said that night upon his knees."

India is so vast that scores of homes are needed, and when a missionary comes to study ours with a view to opening one in her language area, we are very glad. Once a friendly Bishop wrote of wanting to do "something of the sort, if we did not mind." Mind? We had prayed for that very thing with keen desire for years.

But though there is sadness in our hearts because of the many still unreached, yet here as wherever children are loved there is clear air and sunshine; and, of course, there are manifold excitements. Life is exciting when you are five or six, for everything is so extraordinarily new. One of the nursery-songs of the time, "We like new things," used to be sung with a sort of rapture when the bright eyes, which saw so much more than grown-up people's eyes seemed to see, discovered some new thing.

Then there were the ecstatic hours when a small girl changed from a *camasu*, the dress of the bigger littles (the smaller littles have knickers), to a *sãri*, the dress of the grown-up. No one who has heard the gay shout of, "Now we are all grown-up women, and we shall be grown-up women to the end of our lives!" is likely to forget it. Every fold of the adorable *sari* is stroked down and patted, and if you are well loved you are expected to stroke and pat too. The one disadvantage (no pocket) is made up for by the glory of having something to fold round your waist; and into that fold you can tuck anything, even a squirrel.

For squirrels were the first of a long procession of animal friends. Young squirrels have the uncomfortable habit of falling out of their nests, and rats and crows are well aware of this. So there was always a look-out kept for imperilled infants. A squirrel makes a charming pet; it can pick its owner's hand out of any number of other hands, and will snuggle down therein, in the prettiest, most confiding way. Squirrels went to school and even to church with their owners, no one forbidding. It would not have been much use to forbid, for what a squirrel wishes to do, that thing it generally does.

Dear, tiny fieldmice came next, and so something grew to be for which we were very thankful years later, when it was put to the proof. For a circus of performing animals came to a town near by, and, of course, every boy and girl yearned to see a live lion. But when they understood what it must have meant to that lion to be trapped, "trained" to do things unnatural to any animal, and finally carted about in a cage, a prisoner for life, to be stared at by crowds—an abhorrent ordeal to any poor beast—they fully understood why that circus was taboo.

Now that we are what a family is usually meant to be— brothers and sisters, not sisters only—and all caring very much for animals, many things happen which pleasantly anticipate the time when beasts and birds, and we of human kind, will be friends with one another. Even now a boy has a kingfisher, shyest of shy birds, who will come flying down to him from a tree when he calls; a bulbul will light on the shoulder of someone walking along the path. And Jim the myna, who for six years has refused to go off, as most wild birds do, at mating time, welcomes any bird or young creature to his cage, whose door stands open invitingly by day.(A cage is required for most tame things at night, because jungle-cats, rats and snakes do not yet understand our point of view.) The latest story about this bird is that when a guinea-pig went into his cage, he was taken aback for a moment. A Sittie standing by said, "A visitor for you, Jim," and he recovered his manners, bowed as mynas do, and said politely, "Good morning." Even Kut, the big tabby, aged now fourteen years, and Marmalade, so called because

he is marmalade-colour, seem to learn friendliness, and it is not a
"made-up story," but true, that one day Jim, the myna, addressed
Kut thus, "Are you hungry?" and Kut only grunted.

But these are stories of to-day.

5. THE NUGGET

Let a girl's education be as serious as a boy's. You bring up your girls as if they were meant for sideboard ornaments, and then complain of their frivolity. Give them the same advantages that you give their brothers. Teach *them*, also, that courage and truth are the pillars of their being. There is hardly a girls' school in this Christian Kingdom where the children's courage and sincerity would be thought of half so much importance as their way of coming in at a door. And give them, lastly, not only noble teachings, but noble teachers.

Dorothea Beale of Cheltenham, Elizabeth Raikes.

THE simplicities of life have filled most of our pages so far, because, naturally, they come first in the story of the child Kohila. But running through them all like a vein of iron ore was that which this book has set itself to try to tell—the spiritual training of a soul; and in that training truth, loyalty, honour took first place. We were blessed in having some children who seemed to have been born truthful. (It is a mistake to think there are none such east of Suez.) But it was also true that a child might have every jewel of character that you could desire—except truth. We never dared to be off guard there. "Truth once given form becomes imperishable," but let the edges of truth be blurred, and that pure form is very difficult to recover.

When Kohila came, there were about two hundred in the family; there was much to do and there were few to do it, but we had many friends and, where the upbringing of children was concerned, each advised something different. So, as we were not at all self-confident, though very sure of what we wanted, we were sometimes puzzled. Never was a more pertinent fable than that of the father, son and donkey, and we made a cautionary rhyme of the story of the bear and her cub.

Said a baby bear
To his mother,
Which paw shall I move,
This or t'other?
Right or left or all
Four together?
So he stood in doubt
Asking whether,
Front or back should go,
This or t'other;
Do not talk. Just walk,
Growled his mother.

I do not expect that any of our ways were **new**—there is no new thing under the sun ("Is there a thing whereof **men** say, See, this is new? it hath been already in the ages which were before us")—but those ways were new then to most of our friends. And the mother of the children, who was trying, till better help came, to frame a plan for their education, always with the thought of the upper and the nether springs in mind, had only had the training of an evangelist. So everything that could be gleaned, especially from an expert, was noted and pondered, sometimes to be gratefully adopted, sometimes to be discarded. The Home Education Series literature came our way about this time, and was an immense help. (We often wished that Ambleside was not seven thousand miles from Dohnavur.) A few years later the Life of Dorothea Beale of Cheltenham College enlightened and fortified our thoughts.

India has neither a keen sense of historical truth nor a careful affection for accuracy. So we began with true wonder-stories. And nursery-rhymes, whether in Tamil or English, were not about cows jumping over the moon, or tails of poor mice cut off with a carving-knife, or anything of that sort, but jingles made up on the spur of the moment about the common things of homestead, field and garden.

We tried to keep a difference between Sunday rhymes and Monday rhymes, but they sometimes overlapped:

The lizard runs along the ground and then runs up a tree,s
He turns his funny little head and then he looks at me,
He wiggle-waggles up and down and then he looks at me,

chanted Kohila and her set with enthusiasm one Sunday morning, just as we were on our way to the village church, which in those days we attended. Visions of a shocked Pastor's face looking over the low mud wall that separated us from his backyard drew forth a mild remonstrance. "But look," was the instant, triumphant answer, "please look; the lizard's doing it; he's going on doing it!" So we were not too rigid. It would not grieve their Creator if we sang of what His sinless creatures did quite sinlessly on Sunday.

But the children taught us far more than we taught them, and the first lesson they taught us was to be very forgiving. Children are so forgiving that they do not seem even to remember our mistakes and mishandlings, much less do they hoard them up against us. "Are not those chapters in Ezekiel comforting, when we feel our shortcomings, and that we sometimes lead children wrongly?" Dorothea Beale wrote once, perhaps with the American R.V. of Ezek.34.15 in mind, "Because the shepherds made them to err I Myself will be their Shepherd."

We were often helped by those who knew better than we did how to teach: they dropped many a nugget.

"You have written your *t* in two different ways on the blackboard," said a friend who strolled into the nursery schoolroom one day. "Children should see only one way of making a letter." That was a nugget of truth, and we picked it up with thanksgiving and turned it to account in more matters than the making of t's.

For it reminded us that our touch must be steady. To our

heavenly Caleb's, What wouldest thou? we had asked that each might enter into the great *"I thirst"* of Calvary. We had pledged ourselves to work for that, never for anything less; our one aim was that each should be God's missionary, to use a word that should not be limited to any one set of people.

The training of a missionary should begin in the nursery; school should continue it; home should nourish it. All influences should be bent one way. That training should not be perplexed by a mixture of thoughts, but expressed in a single line of conduct, clearly recognised for what it is. In other words, till the life of a child has had time to root, it should not be exposed to various winds (confused or conflicting examples and ideals, different ways of making t's). After it has rooted, let the winds blow as they will. *Then* they will only cause the roots to take a firmer grip.

6. FROM AN OLD PREFACE

For a man's mind is sometime wont to tell him more than seven watchmen, that sit above in a high tower. And above all this pray to the most High, that He will direct thy way in truth. Let reason go before every enterprise, and counsel before every action.

Ecclesiasticus 37: 14-16.

MANY must have noticed how kindly they were helped when they were feeling their way to some decision, even a small decision. Shall we white-wash our wall? that was the not very serious question about the time that Kohila came, for we were building a wall round the children's compound then. Yes, was the expected answer, for to do so is the custom here.

But one Sunday morning, as Kohila and her friends sat in orderly rows in the village church, listening, let us hope, to the sermon, my eyes wandered across through the open church door to our wall, which was then going up. And the earth spoke softly, "I am not white, Let the wall grow up out of me, be part of me." And it was so also with the buildings that the wall enclosed. They were washed with a reddish earth which is sold in our South Indian bazaars, and which is the colour of the ground in this part of the country. (We have even a Red Lake under the hills.) Years later, when I read of the charm of the Cotswold cottages, I understood that the voice of the earth had not misled me that day. We have never regretted that we are, as a colony, not white, delightful as white-wash is in our villages at home, but something that seems to grow out of the soil and "belong."

Often it is a book that helps to guide or to fortify.

How many bored children, I wonder, in the days of long sermons have turned for diversion to the Preface of their Bible—

and found it? "Great and manifold were the blessings, most dread Sovereign"—and "Little Arthur" had said of that same monarch, "He was one of the most foolish and the most mischievous kings we ever had in England and nobody could ever teach him how to behave wisely."

But there is a Bible which does not waste a page on that fulsome twaddle; it prints instead the honest prose which was prefixed to the Version of 1611.

"Zeal to promote the common good, whether it be by devising anything ourselves, or revising that which hath been laboured by others, deserveth certainly much respect and esteem, but yet findeth but cold entertainment in the world. It is welcomed with suspicion instead of love, and with emulation instead of thanks: and if there be any hole left for cavil to enter (and cavil, if it do not find an hole, will make one), it is sure to be misconstrued, and in danger to be condemned. This will easily be granted by as many as know story, or have any experience."

"If we building upon their foundation that went before us, and being holpen by their labours, do endeavour to make that better which they left so good; no man, we are sure, hath cause to mislike us; they, we persuade ourselves, if they were alive, would thank us."

And then, as if to meet half-way a hundred criticisms:—
"The work hath not been huddled up in seventy-two days, but hath cost the workmen, as light as it seemeth, the pains of twice seven times seventy-two days, and more. Matters of such weight and consequence are to be speeded with maturity: for in a business of moment a man feareth not the blame of convenient slackness."

I leave the discerning to discern why I copy these sentences from an old preface.

7. SEEDS OF SONG ARE IMMORTAL THINGS

The Prince of Life was crucified,
He hung upon the bitter tree,
For love of all—for love of me.

The Prince of Life, He rose again.
He triumphed in great majesty,
That I and all might be set free.

The Prince of Life is Heaven's King;
I am the least of things that be;
And yet He says He cares for me.

O Prince of Life, give me Thy love,
The thirst of love that was in Thee,
From Bethlehem to Calvary.

"WHAT fellowship shall the earthen pot have with the kettle? This shall smite, and that shall be dashed in pieces." This sentence fairly expresses life as it really is in a Tamil town or village. There is little fellowship. There are endless feuds and bickerings and bangings of kettles, to the embarrassment of pots. And so almost the first thing both men and women who find their way to us say among themselves, and sometimes to us, is, "What peace!" We have our pots and kettles too. No large community in the Tamil country is without them; but we do not let them disturb the general tranquillity. Gradually it has become known far and wide that our home is a peaceful place, and even in those early days when we took the children out "preaching" as they called it, or just to sing to any who gathered to listen, the listeners did not turn away with, "This is *summa*" (mere chaff of words). They knew there was something behind. As for us, ringing in our hearts always, were the words, If thou forbear to deliver them that are drawn unto

death, and those that are ready to be slain; if thou sayest, Behold,
we knew it not; doth not He that pondereth the heart consider it?
and He that keepeth thy soul, doth He not know it? and shall not
He render to every man according to his works?

Often, long before she knew much more than that she
was very happy, the child of our story and the other children
found themselves talking with the village women, who came
in the evenings to the water-side when the rain had given us
abundance of water. And Kohila would sing with all the
abandon of her loving heart, for no shyness troubled her then.
"It was the young children's singing that drew me to want to
hear the Gospel, and also their happiness;" many a woman, and
many a man, too, has said this to us.

For the East cannot resist song; there is tragedy under
much that looks light-hearted, and joy (like love) draws. So,
often when the waters were out, as we say, we used to sit on the
bank, and the village women would come and listen. "Your
enjoyment is never right till you esteem every Soul so great a
treasure as our Saviour doth ... Who can love too much anything
that God made? What a world this would be were everything
beloved as it ought to be. We should be all Life and Mettle and
Vigour of Love and that would poise us." Our children have been
saved from the depths, for great is His mercy towards them. He
has delivered their soul from the lowest hell, and we cannot be
satisfied with what is so often thought enough. We cannot, God
helping us, rest till to each one the Cross "is a Tree set on fire with
invisible flame, that illuminateth all the world, the flame of Love;
the love in His bosom who died on it."

But the last thing that the world desires is the
illuminating flame. At one village to which we went together there
was a temple where the priests came out in great wrath and bid us
begone. The children did not know all that lay behind that wrath and

their own escape from its dreadful power; or how the one who had taken them to that village had prayed for words of fire to scorch the hearts and consciences of people at home about that lowest hell. "O that my tongue were in the thunder's mouth, then with a passion would I shake the world"—the words are too tremendous to use of most things. They are not too tremendous to use of wrong done to children anywhere. And in a land where one cannot penetrate far without coming upon an appalling callousness about the pain of animals, they often come to mind. Sacrificial killing, to name only one distress, can be very cruel. Protests are made. People who detest cruelty are harrowed, but they are helpless. They know the law. They know that it expressly sanctions any manner of death for any animal if it be done in the name of religion.*

There is only one certain way of ending such infamies. Thank God, there is a way. It is this conviction which makes the smallest opportunity to bring man, woman or child to the Lord Jesus Christ, so precious to His messenger. Among the opportunities which little Kohila shared was the Sunday afternoon children's meeting, when some thirty or forty girls and boys came from the villages near by. Kohila and the other children used to gather flowers for them, for all India loves flowers; and then comfortably sitting on the ground under a tamarind tree, we taught them texts and stories and songs.

After a while we divided up into groups, and each child had her own two or three to whom she taught in the Eastern way, by sing-song repetition, that which she had so lately learned herself. This went on steadily for some months, and then at Christmas we gave the Hindu

---

* Nothing in this Act shall render it an offence to kill any animal in a manner prescribed by religion or religious rites or usages of any race, sect, tribe or class." Section II of the Prevention of Cruelty to Animals Act (Act XI of 1890). Only one who knows India well can begin to imagine what this sentence, protects. Not that we of the West have clean hands. "Research" is a word that covers much. *Lord, how long wilt Thou look on?*

children Christmas cards; and their parents took fright. This was dangerous. The cards were poisoned. A fine dust was somehow introduced into them, and as the children looked at the cards, they would breathe this dust and become Christians. No one had ever seemed to fear that the flowers would be poisoned, so we had not hesitated to give those cards. But now the village elders held a council and forbade the children to come to us any more.

But there is something immortal in seeds of song. One evening, after Kohila had begun her nurse's training, we were walking along the water-side when a young man came up shyly, "Do you remember me? I used to come to the children's meetings under the tamarind tree." And he chanted text after text and sang song after song. And I marvelled afresh at the power of life in the merest thistle-down of song, and more and more we set words of eternal import to any simple tune we could find and committed our seeds to the Winds of God.

8. THERE AROSE A STORM ...
AND HE AROSE

We know that each height, each step, must be gained by patient, laborious toil, and that wishing cannot take the place of working; we know the benefits of mutual aid; that many a difficulty must be encountered, and many an obstacle must be grappled with or turned.

The Ascent of the Matterhorn, Edward Whymper.

Then suddenly there happened one of those trivial things which look like accidents, but I believe are part of the reasoned government of the universe.

The Three Hostages, John Buchan.

Although all the weapons of war change and are ever changing, the main principles remain the same. One of the first of these is that a soldier should be prepared to learn something new from every practical experience of warfare. . .
I pray daily for courage, tranquillity and self-control.

Life of Earl Haig, Duff Cooper.

THIS happy life was soon interrupted. The people who had given Kohila to us, signing a paper to that effect, changed the r mind and wanted her back. We knew that to return her would mean for that dear child destruction and desolation. We could not give her to that, and told them so. Then they brought a criminal case against us.

There was only one way to save her. It was to put her where she would be safe, and if asked to say where that was, refuse to do so. This, of course, would have been a serious offence. And yet we had no choice. For many weeks prison for the one responsible was not a remote, but a very near possibility, and, facing this, we realised how far behind us lies the place where the earliest missionaries stood when they endured shame as a matter of course, for His Name's sake.*

---

* Gold Cord, ch.16, tells another side of this story. At the time the telegram of which that story tells, came to the house, we were gathered

But by the tender mercy of the Lord, the storm blew over us and passed: "When the waves arise, Thou stillest them." And the day came when the friend, who had stood by us so valiantly during that time of threatened trouble, wired to us that the criminal case had been dismissed. No one ever did or ever will know why that happened, for though we had done nothing criminal, it would have been easy to "prove" that we had. And no one knew then, or knows now, why those who wanted to recover the child did not appeal to the Civil Court, as the magistrate advised them to do. Something must have happened to divert their attention from his words. There are no earthly explanations where such things are concerned, and the heavenly reasons are not told us yet. But if it be true—as I believe it is—*that when our prayers are framed upon some word of our God made vital to us* ("some fragment transformed into a supplication"), then we may ask what we will, for we cannot ask in this sense unless we are moved by the Spirit to do so; and though a thousand forbidding Powers arise and declare it shall not be, yet it is done. "The counsel of the Lord, *that* shall stand."

> *Refuge from storm, a Shadow from the heat*
> *Of glowing sand,*
> *Fierce though their blast, the Terrible Ones retreat*
> *At Thy command.*
> *We hear them rage like wind against a wall;*
> *At Thy "Be still," we see them sink and fall.*

---

together to wait upon the God of Deliverances. Years afterwards we read that when the telegram telling of a victory was brought to Admiral Jellicoe he was reading Ps.115: "Not unto us, O Lord, not unto us, but unto Thy Name give the praise." Constantly we find that the true and gallant books of the world meet us where we are or where we want to be; and they speak straight to our heart. We are all one Company, one Fellowship.

If it be true that all good poems are called forth by an occasion, it is true also of the overflow of the heart. Our life has been rich in "occasions" and so our songs have been called forth; and we sing in the ways of the Lord that great is the glory of the Lord.

Before that relieving wire had come, a trivial thing had happened—one of those things that look like accidents, but which are surely "part of the reasoned government of the universe." The child was being taken by boat through the backwaters that run along the western coast of Southern India, when the anxious brother in whose charge she was, heard her matter discussed by some Muslims at the end of the boat. How they knew who she was we never heard, and why they presently began to talk of something else, and thereafter took no notice of her, we never heard; only we know that by "some accident" it was so. And the child was saved.

But till we were sure that all was well, the shy little Kohila had to be hidden away in the heart of the country hundreds of miles distant. And for five months she was sheltered there by friends who were prepared to take any risk to help us. We thanked God for our splendid friends.

Often in those days, when the idea of saving children was a new thing, we had to keep a basket with all the child would require packed ready, and plans had to be made for a journey at a minute's notice. For experience of the uncertainties of Courts had taught us that it was not safe to wait till judgment is given before securing a child's protection. (There was a time when it was impossible to find any safe place in India, or even in Ceylon, and then it was China that sheltered a young girl from the worst that can befall a girl.) We had known what it was to push through "empty" air and feel as though it were crowded with opposing forces—but there were angelic forces there, too; we were not unaware of them. Still, experience had made it impossible to take such attacks lightly. So we thought beforehand, and "took courage in the ways of Jehovah," and to Him we committed our cause, the cause of the helpless, and found comfort in the word that says, *He will carry through the cause,*[*] carry it through with His own right hand; "For what the holy God has purposed who shall frustrate? and who shall turn back His uplifted hand?" [†]

But the law which more than once was almost put in operation against us was a good law, framed to deal with a crime. The work that we were doing had not been thought of when that law was made; it had no choice but to deal with us as malefactors; so we arranged that whatever happened to us there would be no appeal, and we went on quietly taking risks. (Was there ever a war where no one risked anything?) And the old story found a new fulfilment, not once but often, during those years: There arose a great storm of wind ... And He arose and rebuked the wind. He knew how difficult it would have been for the family if the one in charge had been in prison. For in India the custom is instantly to pounce on the under-dog; and here the under-dog would have been the little, defenceless community left unmothered, disgraced.

We learned then that to walk on the water should be the natural thing; our Lord treated it so; and not to be able to walk upon it should be unnatural for a Christian. This is the reverse of the usual thought; but it is true. It is not that we require great faith for this walk when He who is Commander in the waters says, Come, but that our faith is "little" if, seeing the wind boisterous, we begin to sink. "Faith is that which stands upon something which, without faith, could bear no weight." [‡]

---

* Ps.140.12. Delitzsch.   † Isaiah 14.27. LXX.
‡ Editor of *World Dominion*.

It is strange to read in the recently published lives of English statesmen about the tremendous affairs that were piling up on the political horizon during those months. Events, whose reverberations fill the world to-day, were even then in the making, and yet the salvation of this Indian child was our chief preoccupation, and the most engrossing subject of prayer and thought and effort. Two years later the Great War broke out, and for millions of earth's peoples life was never to be the same again.

An incident from that War which is not told in the Life of Earl Haig is so relevant to our story that I tell it here. Professor George Duncan, who was Presbyterian Chaplain at the General Headquarters in France, felt it too sacred for print till Earl Haig had passed into the presence of his Lord.

Whenever the General was near the little wooden hut where the Sunday Services were held, he was always present. But on the day afterwards remembered as Black Sunday, in March 1918, the Chaplain had felt it impossible that he would come. He would be tied to his desk or directing operations. To his astonishment the General did come, calm and resolute as ever. "On the ramparts of Montreuil we shook hands in silence and, scarcely knowing what I said, I expressed the hope that things were not too bad.

Quietly, but reassuringly, he replied, 'They will never be too bad.'

"'No,' I said, 'you who were through Mons and Ypres in the first year will never think anything too bad after that.'

"And then he said, in a language of a kind which I had never heard him use before—for though he lived his religion he did not talk about it—'This is what you once read to us from the Second Chronicles, *Be not afraid nor dismayed by reason of this great multitude; for the battle is not yours, but Gods'*. With these words he passed into the church.

"Perhaps that quotation reveals something of his secret," the Chaplain wrote. "The battle had passed out of human hands, but it was still in God's, and under God it depended on him more than on any man, if defeat was to be turned into victory.

"Little wonder that he came to pray, and, as it happened, on that Sunday evening he did the biggest thing of his career, for, returning to Montreuil after midnight, after a fruitless consultation near Amiens with Marshal Petain, he immediately wired to London urging that steps be taken at once to secure a Generalissimo for the whole Allied front.

"By so doing he made what, for a Commander-in-Chief, was the supreme sacrifice, but the line was saved."*

Those words, *The battle is not yours, but God's* often steadied us. There were times when the loss of a single one pledged to this fight would, it seemed, have led straight to disaster, so thinly spread out was our line. And even now, though we have many more to help, we have also a very much longer line to hold; so conditions do not vary. Why should things be so difficult when our one aim is to fight the battles of our Lord, and do our Father's will? When such a thought came, that wise book *The Pilgrim's Progress* answered us: "Some have also wished that the next way to their Father's house were here, that they might be troubled no more with either hills or mountains to go over; but the way is the way, and there's an end."

---

* " 'At first it was proposed that I should be given the command of the Reserve Armies around Amiens, at the point of juncture between English and French troops.

'Clemenceau agreed.

" But that is not enough," said Haig, "Foch must have command of the whole of the Western Front." '

Marshal Foch, by Raymond Recouly.

9. UNDER THE TREE

The corruptible body presseth down the soul, and the earthly tabernacle weigheth down the mind that museth upon many things.

Wisdom 9.15.

Faint not to be strong in the Lord; that He may confirm you, cleave unto Him: for the Lord Almighty is God alone, and beside Him there is no other Saviour.

Ecclesiasticus 24.24.

UPON a day when anxieties were pressing on all sides, I sat through a hot afternoon under a tree by the wayside, waiting for a bullock-cart which had somehow wandered and left me stranded.

Cloud and mist shadowed the hills, but overhead there was blazing blue, and the tree offered little shade. Its friendliness lay in its great trunk, which made an arm-chair, and sitting on the ground there, I waited.

It was the kind of day the Psalmist had in mind when he wrote about the multitude of his thoughts within him. For a fear had begun to move in us. What if the one whom we very sorely needed was not recovering, but slowly dying? How could we go on without her?* I had been helping her Premie Sittie (Frances Beath) to nurse her in hospital, and was now needed at home to relive Arulai Tara,† who was beginning to be worn out with over-many burdens. What if she broke? Then we should have no one able to undertake responsibility to help with all these children.

And there were little ones for whose sake we were fighting, but, as it seemed, in vain, and everything looked almost impossible,

---

* *Ponnammal* tells of her heroic life and passing into the fuller life.
† *Ploughed Under* tells the story of her childhood and early girlhood.

though, thank God, the thought of giving up never came. But questions did: Shall the throne of iniquity have fellowship with Thee? Why do these things happen, O Lord God of the spirits of all flesh? And this grief, this mist of grief, must it fall in rain?

Presently, as I sat there, words began to sing themselves over to me:

> *Far in the future lieth a fear,*
> *Like a long, low mist of grey,*
> *Gathering to fall in dreary rain,*
> *Thus doth thy heart within thee complain;*
> *And even now thou art afraid, for round thy dwelling*
> *The flying winds are ever telling*
> *Of the fear that lieth grey,*
> *Like a gloom of brooding mist upon the way.*

> > *But the Lord is always kind,*
> > *Be not blind*
> > *To the shining of His face,*
> > *To the comforts of His grace.*
> > *Hath He ever failed thee yet?*
> > *Never, never. Wherefore fret?*
> > *O fret not thyself, nor let thy heart be troubled,*
> > *Neither let it be afraid.*

The second verse left the mist and rain behind: "Wake the voice of joy and health within thy dwelling," was the word now.

The verses appeared to be rather formless, but they were consoling, and to write them down helped through that scorching hour. The only paper at hand was the thin, cheap, brown paper of our Indian bazaars. It was wrapped round a spirits-of-wine bottle which I was taking home. One could not peel the paper off, it was too thin for that, it stuck like skin to the glass; so the writing had to wind round the bottle. It was not a tidy effort, but "When you cannot do what you want to do, do something else" is among the smaller harbour-lights by which we steer, and when this "something else" was finished the wandering bullock-cart trundled up with a gallant jingle of bells, the bottle and I climbed into the cart, and an hour or so later were home.

There immediately crowds of things rushed up and I forgot about the words on the bottle. Nor had I meant them to be kept. They did not seem worth that. But someone retrieved them and another set them to music, so they have survived. And never again on any journey on an Indian road did I pass a tree buttressed in this particular way without being reminded of that day and that comfort.

I have told of it—so very small a thing to tell at all when one considers what great things are happening in the world—because it may be that there are other roads in other lands and streets in many a town set with reminders of times which, if only we would let them remind us, would say, "There, by that turning, as you went into that shop, as you saw that building, or that tree by the wayside, in the multitude of the sorrows that you had in your heart, the comforts of your God refreshed your soul. Fear not therefore, for He who was with you then is with you now." And perhaps the story of my tree may recall to some reader a forgotten consolation.

For He who is the Strength of our heart, and our Portion for ever, does not weary of repeating the words that repetition can only make the more beloved. And He often uses common things— even the trunk of a tree—to recall the music of those words.

PART 2

GIRLHOOD

There your workday toil shall mate
With your prayer, nor desecrate.
Life and faith shall merge, and be
Ringed about as is the tree
By the all-enclosing bark;
Doctrine, worship, shall be one
With the labour daily done.

Brand, Henrik Ibsen.

What matters is that religion should sway our motives, sustain our principles, surround and bathe our spirits like a secret atmosphere as we go about our work. That is religion in common life.

This Torch of Freedom, Stanley Baldwin.

One night on deck it seemed to me that Christ came to me and showed me why we are here, and what the purpose of life really is. It is to make a great decision—to choose between the material and the spiritual, and if we choose the spiritual we must work out our choice, and then it will run like a silver thread through the material.

' Birdie ' Bowers of the Antarctic, George Seaver.

10. CARRYING STONES
AND EARTH AND SAND

"Jesus, Saviour, dost Thou see
When I'm doing things for Thee?
Common things, not great and grand,
Carrying stones, and earth and sand?"

"I did common work, you know,
Many, many years ago;
And I don't forget. I see
Everything you do for Me."

FOR some years it had been impossible to leave the children
in the hot weather, when Europeans usually go to the Hills, so we
had gone together to an upland valley a day's journey from Dohnavur,
where the Forest Department let us use a house they had built there.

We soon overflowed it; and so we searched till we found a
ravine carved out of a mighty forest some three thousand feet above
Dohnavur and within a few hours' walk. "A green thought in a
green shade" that dear place was soon to be to us—Our Forest, the
children called it, feeling possessors of it all when we built our first
house there, still more when some fifty of them helped us to build
another. They saved us pounds in coolie-pay by carrying basket-
loads of building-stuff; and their little brown hands were soon as
sore as ours were, for of course we all worked together, just as
we scrubbed floors together, and indeed did everything we could
together. I have a vivid picture in my mind of a Sittie standing on
the top rung of a ladder, handing up tiles to the masons; while
below strings of children carried the tiles from the heaps where
they were stacked, passing them from hand to hand (or from head
to head, for all were carried on the head). Then they were carefully
hoisted one by one up the ladder by those stationed on its lower

rungs, till they reached the Sittie who supplied the masons. The roof has a large span; it was a relief when at last it was covered.

I cannot remember hearing any grumbling. We left that luxury to the poor coolies, who, after all, had so much more cause than we ever had to be miserable in what they regarded as a waste, howling wilderness. Even when it rained, and all paid help melted like sugar in water, there was nothing but cheeriness, and the children never tired of singing the chanties which we had practised together the week before we went up to the Forest. Most of the fifty were recovering from whooping-cough at the time, and the singing used to be interrupted by paroxysms of that unpleasant malady, but it never quite ceased and work-hours were broken by merry meals (when rain held off) down by the river-bed, where big pots of rice and curry were set among the boulders.

This house—the Jewel House, so called because of the colours of its stones when they were first quarried—was meant to be for the little boys, of whom by this time we had a good many. We planned that they should live there with a Sittie who was devoted to them. For we had found that boys often needed protection, as temple people had uses for them, and so had the Dramatic Societies which abounded in Southern India. When a boy was adopted into either of those communities, all the good in him was turned to the contrary; he had no more chance of growing up pure than a girl had. After long waiting and many perishings of hope we were compelled, as by a Hand upon us, to begin this work.

So the little girls, as the boys were then too small to help, did all that willing children could do to prepare for their younger brothers. Later on Kohila was to nurse some who came to us very fragile, held to life, as it seemed, by a single thread. She saw many grow up strong and fit, ready to be passed on to the Accal, Pappammal, who with her helping Accals, has charge of the little boys' world.

It was by a waterfall below the Jewel House that the answer to the prayer of years came clearly; and the commanding word was spoken, and the sustaining and inspiring word given that made the impossible possible. "The glory of the Impossible"—ever since the beginning of work for girls that phrase had been a bugle-call. It was to become so more and more as the work for boys progressed, till the very word "Impossible" drew the heart on to some new step out on the void which always turned to rock under our feet.

Nine years were to pass before the leader for the boys' work, Godfrey Webb-Peploe, was given. Peace of God is his Tamil name. Long before he came, we had learned that if we pray for the salvation of children we must be prepared to lay down our lives for them, come wind, come weather. Soon after he joined us we had to face a difficult day. We saw "to the bare bone of naked Truth's relentless skeleton" that day. I was thinking of that bare bone when a note came from him quoting Dean Church: "Manliness is not merely courage, it is the quality of soul which frankly accepts all conditions in human life, and makes it a point of honour not to be dismayed or wearied by them." And I knew that all conditions were accepted.

He is faithful that promised. Often, as others followed, brothers born for adversity, comrades born for hard battles, we looked back to that waterfall among the mountains, and great words came to mind like great chords heard in the music of many waters: *A faithful friend is a strong defence: and he that hath found such an one hath found a treasure. Nothing doth countervail a faithful friend, and his excellency is invaluable. A faithful friend is the medicine of life: and they that fear the Lord shall find him. Blessed be the Lord God of Israel, who hath with His hands fulfilled that which He spake with His mouth.*

11. ABOUT THE PATTERN

I do not see how the standard can be carried higher than Christ or his Apostles carry it, and I do not think that we ought to put it lower. I am sure that the habitually fixing it so much lower, especially in all our institutions and public practice, has been most mischievous.

Arnold of Rugby, Arthur Penryn Stanley.

"We try to do without the vision sometimes, and at other times we are half ashamed of owning that we have it, and instead of trying to lift others to see it, go down and meet them in their grey world."

Mrs. Creighton to Dr. Randall Davidson.

BY this time Kohila had almost forgotten the Kinder-garten stage of life, and was a little school-girl in the school called Jeevalia, Place of Life, which is built Indian-fashion round a courtyard. In later years its northern side made the wall for the enclosed garden of the House of Prayer. To that House covered ways lead which are like two long mats of greenery and flowers, if one looks down upon them from the tower where the Prayer-bell chimes are set. From the tower one sees all round, and to the north and west the buildings of the different little worlds, which are in such closely-interwoven relationship that it is impossible to touch a single thread without affecting all. This has its difficulties, but it is worth anything to continue as we began, one family.

There was always abundance of that blessed thing which the old writers must have meant when they called themselves God's merry men. For Sir Walter Scott was exactly right when he said that humour defends from the insanities. "Where do they put the happiness they sang about in church?" a *puzzled* child asked herself as she studied the countenances of the congregation as it streamed out of church one Sunday morning. We did not want our children ever to feel like that. But all through everything ran a single purpose.

When the second generation of children was entering the silent
years, the years of stress,(when unless you hold them fast in faith and
love you lose them, but if you do hold fast you have them for ever), an
Annãchie was given to the family whose prayer for them was this:

> *Give courage equal to the strain,*
> *And hope that will not yield,*
> *But marches fearless in the train*
> *Of warrior-souls, who welcome pain*
> *On Thy stern battle-field.*

But at the time of which I am writing the blessing of such
brother-love was out of sight.

Forgotten things have sometimes a kindly way of
reappearing when they can help, and some rough notes written
before Kohila came to us have lately reappeared. They show what
the influences were which now surrounded her—had, indeed,
surrounded her from the day when she scrambled out of the
bullock-bandy as it stopped at the door of the bungalow, and hid
her shy little face and her mop of curls in our arms.

First comes a word about the one upon whom the
responsibilities of leadership are laid. There is only one name for
that one: *Servant of all.*

Then about those who were to be welcomed as fellow-
workers the word was, *There went with him a band of men whose hearts*
God had touched. So a kindly willingness to help was not enough.
Difficult circumstances would overset that, other claims would rise
and pull away the one upon whom we had begun to count. There
must be the Touch of God concerning the children in peril; it must
be the Ordination of His hands for this special service, the proof
of which is nothing spectacular, but just a quiet assurance that the
servant is following the Will of the Master. Only that Touch, that

Ordination would ensure that there would be no looking back, and no desire to build in wood, hay, stubble, but in the costliest materials of all—gold, silver, precious stones.

For we saw it as a life-work. *We ought to lay down our lives.* That cut out at a stroke all "buts." all reserves, all non-essentials. It meant loving and serving, never tiring of loving and serving, even unto the end.

Then comes a sentence about the knitting of the Spirit, which neither death, nor life, nor things present, nor things to come, can ever unravel. *If ye be come unto me to help me, mine heart shall be knit unto you.* "Soul and soul together, in a mind which is unity itself."*

Such knitting will mean that we shall be one in work and the work will be one: *Then David consulted with the captains of thousands and hundreds, and with every leader.* Fearless confidence will be the very substance of our life together, just as flawless loyalty will be the hall-mark of its quality. This is only possible if there be such confidence, each in each, that no whisperer can ever come between, nor the shadow of a doubt ever rise.

There was a word about what we willed and what we nilled. What we willed was to co-operate with our Lord in saving the children from the grasp of the dark powers; and, His good Spirit enabling us, to prepare for His service ardent lovers, true warriors. What we nilled was to be satisfied with the usual, cool, respectable, conventional type of Christians—it would not have seemed worth laying down our lives to multiply the number of these. So each one of us must have the burning heart of an evangelist: "By one who loveth is another kindled." That fire must never go out.

There separated themselves unto David into the hold to the wilderness men

---

* Phil. 2 : 3 Moule.

of might, and men of war fit for the battle, that could handle shield and buckler, whose faces were like the faces of lions, and were as swift as the roes upon the mountains; a great host like the host of God—there we saw our Pattern in terms of soldiership.

It came to pass, as the trumpeters and singers were as one, to make one sound to be heard in praising and thanking the Lord and when they lifted up their voice with the trumpets and cymbals and instruments of musick, and praised the Lord, saying, for He is good; for His mercy endureth for ever: that then the House was filled with a cloud even the house of the Lord—that was our Pattern in terms of musical harmony. Nothing less than this resolute and harmonious whole must ever satisfy our hearts.

If this way of life be criticised, "What is that to thee? Follow thou Me," If it be called unpractical, show, by living it, that it is practical. We cannot love one another too much, for He said, "Love one another as I have loved you." We cannot set the standard too high, for it is not ours to move about as we will: it is our Lord's, and He has set it high. If any turn away and leave us, we must not be surprised, as though some strange thing happened unto us. (Will ye also go away?) The disciple is not above his master, nor the servant above his Lord. But let be what be, ours must be that largeness of heart even as the sand that is on the sea-shore. Refuse to be petty; refuse to take offence; refuse to talk. Learn to dwell in silence with Him who, when He was exposed to the utmost provocation, opened not His mouth—thus the recovered notes.

All of us—we were only a very few then, but all of us who were here—were like a knot that nothing could untie where identity of thought on these matters was concerned, and also in the kind of love which many waters cannot quench, neither can the floods drown it.

*　　*　　*　　*　　*

As I write, years after the day when these words were written, a letter comes from one of our Fellowship who is in the Forest, quoting Dr. Arthur Way's rendering of Phil.2.2 (as well as Bishop Moule's which helped us long ago), *One in purpose, cherishing the same love, one in soul and animated by the same aspirations.* So we go forward by the grace of God—not as though we had already attained, but trusting Him "who will evermore put His finishing touches" to that which He, He only, began when He showed us this Pattern on the Mount, and made us as though we were leaves together on a tree blown by the same breath of wind.

12. HOW WE WERE HELPED

God—let me be aware!
Stab my soul fiercely with another's pain.
Let me walk, seeing horror and stain.
Let my hands, groping, find other hands.
Give me the heart that divines and understands.
Flood me with knowledge, drench me with light.

- Teichmer.

Writing to a young teacher about preparation for Scripture classes Dorothea Beale said: "I used to prepare my lessons on my knees. You would find it a help, I think, to do this sometimes."

AT that time Dohnavur was at the end of everywhere, an ideal place if one was in India for the sake of Indian people and eager to give every waking hour of the twenty-four to them. There were no motor-buses, no motor-cars, no motor-cycles. Eight or nine hours' trail in a bullock-cart across a hot plain did not sound enticing, and few were enticed. So we had no parties of sightseers rushing in, "just to be taken round the place," and we were free to live for our children and the people of the villages. We were very grateful for our liberty, and used it to the full.

With us during some of those early years was a friend who had been in the University Settlement at Bombay and had not been strong enough to work there. She helped us as long as strength lasted, and then, some years after the Jeevalia was built, we were given two sisters who were one with us in all our thoughts.* Both had been deeply moved about the wrong done to young children. Both had walked "seeing horror and stain."

---

* Edith Naish; and her sister Agnes, of Westfield College.

The younger sister, in her great longing to stir others to care, had written to friends at home a year before she came to us: "How can I help you to realise it? Even we who are out in the work here, stand only on the edge of the darkness; we do not live in it, as the children do. I think of two fit symbols of it—sights familiar to our Hindu children—the one a black, elephant-headed god with swollen body, ever decorated with fair oleander blossoms that intensify his grotesque ugliness, the other the figure of a female demon crunching a child between her teeth. Here we have personified the darkness of heathenism, its sensuality, and its crushing of the sweet child-nature." This new comrade whom we gratefully welcomed had had fifteen years of educational work in India before she joined us and had clear thoughts about what was, and what was not worth doing. And because she was a keen evangelist, and could hardly pass a peasant-woman on the road without getting into talk with her about the things of God, her chief thought was to fit our children to be evangelists.

Hers, too, was that blessed gift of the teacher, the Giver; it was no effort, but just natural to her to lay her mind alongside the mind of the youngest child she taught, and she dearly loved to give her best to quite little ones. Of all her classes, her Bible-classes made the deepest mark; she was steeped in Bible lore, and drew her students far out of the shallows into those deep waters that, like the river of Ezekiel, are waters to swim in. All that could shed light on the Book she welcomed, and taught her little students to welcome that she might make them know the certainty of the words of truth. And in her teaching there was never that casual mixing up of texts which even in the best daily text-books can be so trying: *It shall greatly helpe ye to understand Scripture, if thou mark not only what is spoken or wrytten, but of whom, and to whom, with what words, at what time, where, to what intent, with what circumstances, considering what goeth before and what followeth,* Wycliffe's often-quoted words are true.

The elder sister also taught in the Jeevalia for a time, turning the generous light of a well-stored mind on those young, opening minds. And although we were bound in honour not to be disobedient to the heavenly vision, we were constantly and marvellously helped. One by one others joined us who would never have given their lives for any lesser vision. So the children had before them that which we did most ardently desire they should become. "Whatever is put in the fire will be of the colour of fire," say the Tamils. "The cord that ties the flowers takes the perfume of the flowers."

From our earliest beginnings we had a few simple customs. Every Monday morning we repeated together I Cor. 13 in Tamil and in English. When Dr. Way's version of the Epistles came out all were keen to read that chapter. His rendering of v.8, *Love's petals never fall*, charmed the flower-loving children. They engraved the words on their brass vessels, worked them into raffia baskets, and printed them on strips of ribbon for their friends.

Then there were the holiday texts which were always repeated on the first day of the holidays: "Look not every man on his own things, but every man also on the things of others. Bear ye one another's burdens, and so fulfil the law of Christ." And on the first morning of term we had our special school-song. To the more thoughtful this song recalls the story told to illustrate one of its verses. The king of Egypt carried away Solomon's golden shields, and Solomon's son made in their stead brazen shields. To show brass instead of gold is a Tamil synonym for insincerity.

> *Set our foundations on the holy hills;*
> *Our city found*
> *Firm on the bed-rock of the Truth; our wills*
> *Settle and ground.*
> *Cause us to stand to our own conscience clear,*
> *Cause us to be the thing that we appear.*

That prayer looks back to the rock where it was quarried. And as I have so far said nothing of the Book viewed as a treasure-mine of stories for children, (taking it for granted that the reader knows all that could be said about that), I will copy some fine words from *The Pentateuch and Haftorahs* edited by The Chief Rabbi, Dr. Hertz. He writes of those ancient stories:

"They are absolutely irreplaceable in the moral and religious training of children. The fact that, after having been repeated for three thousand years and longer, these stories still possess an eternal freshness to children of all races and climes, proves that there is in them something of imperishable worth. There is no other literature in the world which offers that something.

"Not by means of abstract formulae does it [Bible history] bring God and duty to the soul of man, but by means of *lives* of human beings who feel and fail, who stumble and sin as we do; yet who in their darkest groping, remain conscious of the one true way—and rise again."

13. DESERVE MORE RATHER THAN WIN MORE

"Shall we try to deserve more rather than to win more?" said Miss Beale when she quoted the phrase of the Roman senate, ("He deserved well of his country") to some children—not of Cheltenham—who were to receive prizes. It well expresses her feeling about rewards. They should grow out of the work; should be some fresh privilege of service. Hence her indifference to prizes in the College.

Life of Dorothea Beale, Elizabeth Raikes.

In the holidays, and also in term, there is a great deal of what we call Helping-Work done: cooking which all take in turn, cleaning of rice-vessels, husking of rice, and various sundries, such as picking tamarind-fruit, pulping it, salting it and packing it in boxes for use in curry-making. There are hard seeds in the pods, and each child has a stone or a small hammer to break the seeds, so that they can be roasted and boiled and used for cattle-food. Sometimes there is a large crop of young palmshoots, and then even the smallest child can help in peeling them. They are boiled like potatoes, but taste like nothing but themselves. Such work was often done near the great old tamarind which is close to the Jeevalia. Long ago that tree was shamed. Demons were worshipped under its shadow, but it has forgotten all about that, and the children never saw it. Once a little girl who loved the tree had a tamarind-tree song, and she used to sing it at the top of her voice as she stood on its highest bough, only her head and shoulders appearing above the green.

Besides the daily duties of tidying up and watering the plants, holidays give chances to learn *"to buthil"* (do something instead of another, so as to give the other a rest). Little Jeevalia girls go to the nurseries then, and learn how to help their Accals.

Following our Pattern meant that we could not come under the Government curriculum, and though that has given us release from cramming for public examinations, yet the demand made on the teacher has been in some ways all the greater. But a true teacher is a Giver; the Giver lives to give, and we had the blessing of a large liberty and a clear goal. So we had what to us was great gain: we were free to draw all our cares and studies this way—the way that pointed straight to the unhampered leading of our childeren to service for others, untarnished by earthly thoughts. The Reward of Service is the joy of that service.

We never had prizes. The children would have been (and still would be) astonished if any one suggested that they should be given something for receiving what their patient Givers had given to them. Reward for any kind of service never came into our scheme of things, except the reward of giving pleasure or help. The great reward, this was always made clear, was to be trusted with harder, more responsible work.

And now that we are reaping from this sowing, we are very grateful. Some few have not understood, and walk elsewhere in different ways, but far more have rejoiced us by growing up to follow the happy heavenly pattern. And the pleasant sound of love has gone out over all this country-side, so that the very sight of our Dohnavur colours suggests loving help to any who chance to see them anywhere.

A short time ago this was kindly brought home to us. Our bacteriologist was driving the Ford car through a Hindu town. The men's hospital colours are purple and mauve, and the moment these colours were seen by some one in trouble there, he ran home, "I saw the colours of the Place of Healing. Someone from there is here, so there are friends near who will help us even though we have no money at all." And that led to help being given to a family in great distress.

It is the same with the Blues, as the brothers in other work are called because of their colours. It is the same with girls whose colours, if they are working for the ill, are well known and stand for integrity as well as love. This was tested by one not long ago who tried to slip a gift into a nurse's hand. "And gradually," as one of the older Indian members of the Fellowship said lately, "it is becoming understood that there are no private gains made here, no boy or girl wearing our colours will accept a tip; this is making a great difference in the feeling of the people. They know where they are when they come to us. They know they can count on not being fleeced in private. Yes, *character* is the thing we must make, by the grace of God."

And we say so too.

But to attain is not the work of a day, and many must in truth lay down their lives if these things are to be. (Do we not sometimes forget that St. John who said, "We ought to lay down our lives for the brethren," laid his life down in the daily difficult living of unrecorded years?) And yet though, "Not as though I had already attained," is always our word, we do, with Julian of Norwich, rejoice: "I understood that we may laugh in comforting of ourselves and joying in God for that the devil is overcome."

Ours, not his, is the winning side.

14. YOU HAVE COME
TO LEARN HOW TO READ

With regard to younger boys he [Arnold] said,"It is a great mistake to think that they should *understand* all they learn; for God has ordered that in youth the memory should act vigorously, independent of the understanding—whereas a man cannot usually recollect a thing unless he understands it." But in proportion to their advance in the school he tried to cultivate in them a habit not only of collecting facts, but of expressing themselves with facility, and of understanding the principles on which their facts rested. You come here, he said, not to read, but to learn how to read.

Arnold of Rugby, Arthur Penryn Stanley.

BUT that day was distant when Kohila first went to school, and though she was naturally happy, "she was often downhearted because she found this and that lesson difficult, and I have often heard her praying about it," a school-fellow writes, "and in the end, whatever it was, she learned that lesson. She never gave in to anything, but always went through with whatever she began to do, and what she said she would do, that she did." For she was not fond of being conquered. "The difficult is that which can be done immediately; the impossible that which takes a little longer," would have been her feeling, though she could not have put it so tersely.

In the end Kohila understood that the chief purpose of school was to teach her to love wisdom and knowledge, and to nurture that attitude of mind which makes one not ashamed of not knowing, but only of appearing to know when one does not. "Profess not the knowledge which thou hast not"—we tried to teach our children to honour that word.

A friend who understood our desires for them came with us when she could to the Forest in the hot - weather holidays. She lived contentedly in a jungle hut, so jungly that pattering little footsteps could be heard round it at night, and once a monitor walked in; and once (but she was not there then) a tiger-cub came to the porch and gazed in astonishment at a three-year-old girl who gazed in astonishment at him. In this hut our friend told Greek stories to a group of girls called the Readers. They were a little older than Kohila, but the stories were passed down from group to group afterwards, and helped to enlargement of mind; and her wise talks with one and another are often remembered and quoted.

Once what we call a Yãró story was going round - a story, that is, which you cannot trace to its root, for each one you question says, Yãro (someone or other, I don't remember who) told it to me. At last we thought we had run it to earth, for a girl then a Reader was supposed to have started it. "I am a Reader," was her indignant response, "Readers have something better to think about. *They* don't start Yãró stories!"

In the evenings of what we call our cold weather, when it is often wet, the older girls used to gather for that marvel of the time, the gramophone. If a guest who happened to be with us began to talk during the music, they were abashed, and we had difficulty in distracting them from the offence. For they had been brought up otherwise: "Hinder not musick. Pour not out words where there is a musician, and show not forth wisdom out of time."* No child of Dohnavur has ever heard of music as an accompaniment to conversation.

At other times we had books—the most nourishing we could find. (Blessed be books, the distilled essence of action and thought.) And there were other influences, each small in itself, which played a part in the shaping of character.

When the children were very little, each "had a star of her own," or a whole constellation, whose track she watched across the sky, and each had a country about which she gathered all she

---

* Ecclesiasticus 32.3,4. First half of second century B.C., or perhaps earlier.

could. Kohila's was South Africa. There were also those "Ceremonies of Joy" which a family makes for itself. Chief perhaps among them, apart from Christmas, was the Easter-Day greeting and song in God's Garden, and Communion under the tree that stands at the entrance of that garden.

Once a year—but this was much later—the Annāchie, whose name means Peace of God, devised many new interests. Among these was a paper of questions on General Knowledge. This was a holiday pleasure. Girls and boys alike enjoyed it. They were allowed to search any books that they thought would help them to find the answers, a plan that led to careful reading. Kohila was one of those who worked for that paper, and her last answers are marked 98.5 per cent.

The questions were what they called themselves, delightfully general: they dealt with ancient and modern history, geography, inventions, discoveries, temperatures (of human being, animal and bird), boiling- and freezing-point, authorship of hymns, postage to different countries, coinage of different countries and important recent events and their influence on nations.

15. FORGIVEN FROM EGYPT EVEN UNTIL NOW

Who can disentangle that twisted and intricate knottiness? Foul is it: I hate to think on it, to look on it. But Thee I long for, O Righteousness and Innocency, beautiful and comely to all pure eyes, and of satisfaction unsating.

Confessions of St. Augustine.

Nothing is more touching than the penitence of children, when they find that we have seen the good which is hidden, and not only the evil that comes forth; that we know, not only what is done, but what is resisted.

Life of Dorothea Beale, Elizabeth Raikes.

ONE sad little story belongs to Kohila's school days. At that time the children had vegetable and fruit gardens of their own, as well as many flowers. The fruit and vegetables were sold to our Indian housekeeper Rachel, who conscientiously gave no more than the market price for them.

The coppers were collected in a small clay vessel with a slit in the top. Each set of children had one of these. Once a year the family assembled in the room where I am writing now. Closer than ever were sardines in a tin, squeezed into one solid encircling bunch, or wreath of bunches, there they sat, seething with excitement, and watched while one of the brothers solemnly smashed the vessels set in the centre of the circle, and poured out the contents in a heap on the floor. There was a smothered ecstasy in that smashing. Things were not usually lawfully broken, and here were several dozen hard, round, red clay balls put there for that very purpose. There was never a whisper during this ceremony, or during the less absorbing one which followed; for the tiny copper coins were counted twice over, and the amount was written down and declared.

And then for a minute there was babel, as everybody suggested people to whom the money should be given.

Kohila was very much in earnest about her garden, and one day she stayed among her plants instead of going to school, and gave an excuse which was not true. A school-fellow found her an hour or two later, "and she wept and wept as if her heart would break. The background of this thing was just her love for helping poor people. But in the end she was straightforward about every little thing."

A child, thank God, is not drawn out at full tension all the time, so a dear and sunny little face may be all that anyone sees, and yet a few hours earlier storms of passion or of distress may have been boiling up in the heart of that child, or she may have been feeling misjudged, misunderstood.

> Deem the best in every doubt
> Till the truth be tried out,

is the modernised inscription on an English bronze jug dating from the time of Richard II. All who have to do with children know the importance of these words.

*   *   *   *   *

Will any mother, I wonder, read this story—a mother who is absent from her children, in presence, not in heart? And is she, I wonder, broken by the longing to be with them in the old way? There are times when no words touch so nearly as Job's, "Oh that I were as in months past, when my children were about me!" Perhaps some precious child this very hour is a Peter who has gone out and wept bitterly. And you cannot reach your Peter you cannot comfort, perhaps you cannot even know. If others to whom those beloved children are also "own" are with them, that indeed is heart's-ease; and yet you love, and love cannot help longing. We were made so.

Only a few minutes ago I came to the place where I could write no more, and with that desperate sense of the need of heavenly succour which some will understand, I turned to the Book that stood upon the book-rest beside me. The pages fell open of their own accord as it were, at the end of the third Gospel, and the words that met me—*ran* to meet me—were these, "And it came to pass, while He blessed them, *He was parted from them.*" He was parted from them: He has been on this road before us. On every road, even on this road, I see His foot-prints. And He of whom it is written, "Thou understandest my thought afar off," says, perhaps not for the first time, "Thou art sore troubled in mind for their sake. Lovest thou thy beloved better than He that made them?" And I said, "No, Lord."

> We may very safely say, "No, Lord"; for
> The Lord has many a way
> That His children little think of,
> To send answers when they pray.
> *He had finished all she failed in—*

the words come from the Tuscany legend that tells of Suora Marianna, a tired old nun who was nursing a young mother for whom the doctor could do nothing. One night she prayed earnestly that the mother might be healed for the sake of her baby. And then she began to prepare a meal to have ready for the mother in the morning. "Good Lord, help me, only help me through the night," was her heart's cry, for if she failed who would tend the mother? And then, worn out, she fell asleep with her head leaning against the wall, and the food set on the fire of fir-wood.

She woke startled and dismayed. But the fire had not gone out, nor had the food been spoiled; for there by the hearth-stone at her feet stood a little Child. "And a glory shone about Him that was not the firelight glow," and the food on which so much depended was ready for the mother. *"He had finished all she failed in."*

Countless times these simple words have been comfort to the writer. May they be comfort to some reader now.

Even as the words are written, Seela, the Accal who took Kohila into her room when the first bewildering grief that touched the child's life came to her—a later chapter will tell of it—remembers how sensitive Kohila's conscience was about sin of any kind. "She felt it bitterly. It was never a little thing to her. When I took her after her own Accal left us, I found her weak about truth but longing to be strong." "For the holy spirit of discipline will flee deceit, and will not abide when unrighteousness cometh in," and, young though she was, Kohila wanted the Holy Spirit of Discipline to rule her life.

Often in her story we come upon signs that show how her Saviour was guarding that which He had redeemed. He never let her become insensitive—it was always the thought of what He had suffered that she might be forgiven "from Egypt even until now" that broke her down.

> My Lord, my Love, came down from Heaven,
>   With sharp wild thorn they hurt His brow,
> Or ever He could say, "Forgiven,
>   From Egypt, even until now."
>
> My Lord, my Love, was sorely riven:
>   His pure soul He to death did bow,
> That He might say to me, "Forgiven,
>   From Egypt, even until now."
>
> O Love, that Thy poor child hath shriven,
>   I know not why, I know not how,
> Help me to live as one forgiven,
>   From Egypt, even until now.

For "full preciously our Lord keepeth us when it seemeth to us that we are near forsaken and cast away for our sin and because we have deserved it. But our courteous Lord willeth not that His servants despair, for often nor for grievous falling: for our falling hindereth not Him to love us."

Among our oldest Accals is Pearl, Pearl the Faithful. On her fortieth Coming-day she came to me that we might give thanks for forty unbroken years of service together. And she saw Kohila's story in the making, and fingering the pages lovingly she said, "That was a child who was pure of heart indeed. I was ill myself when she was being trained to nurse, so I watched her as a sick person watches a nurse. And I saw her tender to all, not to the good only, but to all. She gathered all into her love."

Are there any so tender as those who have failed and been forgiven, and then full preciously have been kept?

16. THE HALF-HOUR

Christ's statement that "the Sabbath was made for man" has been interpreted to mean that the day might be treated like Saturday afternoon; or its evening like any other evening in the week. But how if the Sabbath was made for man to enable him to tune in to the Power Station of the Infinite? No limitations can be placed on the possibilities that may flow from that Source.

Sir Charles Marston.
(From the Conclusion to his study on the excavations of Lachish).

LONG before Kohila or any of her friends were thought of, a child had listened to the talk of the sailors who looked after the little yachts that were moored near the shore of Strangford Lough. The good smell of salt water, the good sight of honest faces and rough blue jerseys, the sound of lapping water are to this day mixed in her mind with those talks which often dealt with greater things than boats.

There was a rumour of a new Bible, a revised Bible. This was very disturbing. It would mean, among other things, changes in the Psalms of David. The child heard somebody say earnestly that what was good enough for David was good enough for him. The new revivalist hymns which were just then coming into use at meetings, never, of course, in church, were discussed. The paraphrases "were Scripture right enough; but them hymns!"

The child had her private opinions. Even hymns had their points. The recent weekly Prayer-meeting had chanced to have as its *motif* our departure from this world. And she had carefully counted the various things which, according to the hymns, you were supposed to say at that exact moment. This occupation had helped to pass the time, though how a dying person could say so many things at once, had puzzled her. With one of those remarks she had heartily concurred.

71

I'll sing while flying through the air
Farewell, farewell, sweet hour of prayer.

The "sweet hour" must, of course, mean the Wednesday
evening Prayer-meeting of the church to which she belonged.

The pent-up or unlawfully-expanded energies during the Sunday
morning sermon, with its "firstly, secondly, thirdly, finally and in
conclusion"; the ripples of resentment that flowed towards the
unheeding pulpit if the benediction were changed from its briefest
form to its longest; the unexpected pleasure of lighting on George
Herbert's, "He that getteth patience and the blessing that preachers
conclude with hath not lost his pains"—these were the recollections
which lay behind our habit of short Services.

There was silence in heaven about the space of half an hour. Even
There, this, the ultimate act of adoration, was only for about half an
hour. Metaphor? poetry? Be it so, it taught us this: never forget that the
human should not be drawn out like a piece of elastic and held so, for
too long at a stretch. The only exception is when a special outpouring
of the Spirit sweeps like a wind through a community. Then clocks
cease to matter and hours pass like minutes.

Remembering, too, how often song, in spite of a few
exceptions, had carried heavenly thoughts to the heart of a child who
was all one longing to be out of doors again, we had much more
singing than is (or then was) usual. And often, unheard by any human
ear, the second verse of one of the paraphrases the old sailor had
approved changed its pronouns, and sang its lovely lines as a prayer for
these children of India so quickly growing up to face the journey in this
perplexing land:

Through each perplexing path of life
Their wandering footsteps guide;
Give them each day their daily bread,

And raiment fit provide.

O spread Thy covering wings around,
　　Till all their wanderings cease,
And at their Father's loved abode
　　Their souls arrive in peace.

The Half-Hour set apart from all other Half-Hours early on Sunday mornings for just one purpose may seem too simple a thing to write about, and yet Kohila and her generation of children often spoke of it as something that coloured their lives and helped to shape them. We had no sermonising then. It was not meant to be a Gospel Service or for teaching. The teaching of Scripture was at other times. It was just a time when we gathered to rejoice unto Him with reverence. So we met only to worship, and to adore Him who is too little adored.

Some of the young English workers who were studying the language were hardly able to follow in Tamil; and many of our children were learning English, and we wanted them to have the freedom of the language. So the worship was in English. The Sittie who taught the children to sing softly—never in the usual shrill, Indian way—filled the singing part of that Half-Hour with sweetness. "My lips shall be fain when I sing unto Thee and so will my soul whom Thou hast delivered," the words come to me as I think of the singing that meant so much to that Half-Hour.*

We began with a minute's silence, broken by something quiet and worshipful. Then we had prayer, "O God, forasmuch as without Thee we are not able to please Thee," or one framed on a word from

---

* Apart from the great hymns of the Church Universal, we have songs that belong to the life of our family. We owe more than we can say to our friends who have written music for them or harmonised the melodies which members of the Fellowship have written. Most of these are still making music on earth and would rather not be named.

the Book of Wisdom, *Grant unto us, O Lord our God, that we may keep holily the things that are holy and ourselves be hallowed,* or some other short petition, and our Lord's prayer very slowly, as surely such mighty words should be said. Midway in the Half-Hour there was silence (How is it that silence is often so much more moving than speech?) and after that the glorious, "Therefore with angels and archangels and with all the company of heaven."

There were joyful days when we had returned happy and well from the Forest, and then we used to sing the Song of the Three Children because of the words about the Green Things upon the Earth; and at Christmas, of course, there were carols, and at Easter, Easter hymns and versicles. Always, as I have said, the very sweetness of that Half-Hour was gathered into the singing which lifted us all as only music can, and carried us Otherwhere; for there is something in music, "something of Divinity more than the ear discovers."

Near the end we always had the prayer, "Grant, we beseech Thee, merciful Lord, to Thy faithful people pardon and peace"; for who has gone through even half an hour's worship without feeling, as it closes, the need of pardon because of wandering thoughts that need not have been? The prayer for the quiet mind rested our hearts; for life was crowded and clamorous in those days, as indeed it often is still. Then came the great Amen of the eavenlies *(Blessing, and glory, and wisdom, and thanksgiving, and honour, and power, and might, be unto our God for ever and ever, Amen),* which for many years has united us with the Unseen Family; and then, still kneeling, we sang our last prayer, which was often one that falls into stillness like the voice of a hushed child—"Grant us Thy peace —Thy peace."

But one is making music in the Heavenlies, and we feel free to speak of her—Mary Dobson of the Missionary Settlement for University Women, Bombay. She found the music for one of our children's Passion-week Songs as she walked up and down a little room in Jerusalem.

Many a time through the thronged hours of the week the thought of that Half-Hour laid a peaceful hand upon us. Even the careless little school-girls seemed to feel some of its influences following them on gentle feet and gentling them. A word of reminder hardly ever failed to find response.

The Half-Hour continues, exceedingly enriched by the Annãchies who lead it in our House of Prayer. But it retains its first thought of worship, thanksgiving and the adoration of love. The words of man are not much heard; the leader usually weaves into one web some great thought of his God, by reading, with little or no comment, Scriptures that bear upon that thought. And still the family feels as it used to feel, only I am sure more and more as the years pass, the hallowing power of that Half-Hour.

17. PORANA

Then was Christian glad and lightsome, and said, with a merry heart, "He hath given me rest by His sorrow, and life by His death." Then he stood still a while to look and wonder; for it was very surprising to him, that the sight of the Cross should thus ease him of his burden.

The Pilgrim's Progress.

ONE of our nursery trellises is green with porana all the year round. But once a year after rain it blossoms suddenly in masses of snowy white. The prayer of many a child used to be, "Let the porana open on December 16," for that day was a special birthday, and after the delirious excitement that used to begin long before dawn, the next event was always to go to the porana trellis, and if you were small, to dance up and down the path shouting, "Porana! Porana!" as if the flower did not know her own name.

In the evening of that day there was a meeting for the whole family. Like the Half-Hour, this has been continued, and becomes more and more a force among us.

When Kohila was eleven years old, we spent some time on the two days before the meeting in thinking about the pleading words in the Song of Songs, *Let Me see Thy countenance, let Me hear Thy voice.* And that year with the blossoming of the porana flower, something blossomed in the heart of Kohila, and she and two others in her room (one of whom became her fellow-worker on the medical side) did definitely respond to that call.

One of her friends marked those words in the Song of Songs in her Bible that evening, and she remembers how in the quiet time which follows the birthday meeting, when the older help the younger, individually or in little groups, those three gave themselves to the Lord Jesus Christ to be His for ever. And then we gathered together again to praise His name, and to pray for the keeping of the Lord for all who had given themselves to love the Lord their God, and to walk in His ways and to keep His commandments, and to cleave unto Him and to serve Him with all their hearts and with all their souls. Then, with His blessing upon them, we sent them away; and they went to their rooms.

In the following year we began to have meetings, when any who had found help and wanted to pass that help on to others could do so. But among the forty-six names entered in an old record, each with a verse written alongside, Kohila's does not appear. She was still a curled-up kitten; and though she could purr, and did, she had not broken through the folds of shyness that held her. And as there is nothing more fatal than to hustle souls, she was not hustled; the porana opens on the appointed day.

When, at about seventeen, she left school and passed into the work, she was no scholar, but she cared much for books (she had been trained to care for them), and she had a friendly way of copying out anything that helped her and passing it on to others. Often this sweetened life for her friends, "For good words are honeycombs, and the sweetness thereof is a healing of the soul."

She never had what the Cumberland folk call grimly "a determination of words to the mouth"; there are worse lacks than that; but she knew how to find her Saviour in the Writings she had been taught so carefully. "For Jesus, that is all soothfastness, is hid, and covered therein, wound in a soft sendal" (silken stuff), as *The Scale* says, and the seeker finds Him and in quiet ways leads others to find Him. And though she was far from perfect (not many of us are perfect at seventeen), there were some who saw the Lord Jesus, Lover of souls, as they looked at her loving life, looked through it, rather, as through a window at Another. "It is enough for a window that it be transparent."

"Next to helping people, what do you think was her greatest pleasure?" I asked one of her girl-friends. "I think it was singing," she answered. "She sang a great deal." Our Singing Sittie had taught the children the many out-of-door songs which belong specially to them and to their forest and sea. One of the greatest treats was, and is, a Singing Evening. And one of the happiest memories of Forest times is the sound of singing coming up from the path among the trees, or from some grey old rock half smothered in green. Saturday evening was given partly to sweeping the woodland paths and early on Sunday morning we used to hear one and another singing,

> *O hush of dawn, breathe through the air*
> *   And fill the heart in me;*
> *Still is this mountain-land, as where*
> *   God's footsteps be.*

> *And can it be He walks these woods,*
> *   These paths that we have swept?*
> *Then may my heart with all her moods*
> *   Be holier kept.*

> *For not to this dear place belongs*
> *   Aught but the good and gay:*
> *Be all my thoughts like wild birds' songs*
> *   On this Thy day.*

But there were songs about tigers and monkeys and the pool and all manner of every-day simplicities. Thank God He has made us so variously-minded—as various, indeed, as His creation, with its endless and ever-unfolding wonders and delights.

THE PHOTOGRAPHS

When the Lord opened the way for the reprinting of 'Kohila' here in India, we were faced with a dilemma; "What shall we do about photographs?". It was not thought that the old sepia ones would have much appeal for a new generation of readers, yet how could we use present-day pictures to illustrate a story and events that took place over sixty years ago? Eventually, it was felt that it could be done, because so many of the things referred to are still part of our life here, and the fact that the pictures portrayed a different generation, in another era, need not mean that they were untrue or irrelevant.

We hope you will enjoy these glimpses into the life of our Family and that they will provide a colourful and helpful setting for Kohila's story.

"There is nothing daintier than a little girl in a sari" - (ch.1)

(Coming Day Celebrations)

My Birthday
has come
round at last!

Everyone shares the birthday-girl's joy

We want our brass vessels to shine like gold

Swings are fun!

Children playing around the Clock Tower

The
Timothys'
help is
always
appreciated

ith happy memories" (ch.3)
'Rose of sunset'

or blossoming trees

Flame of the Forest

Laburnum

"There are always the Mountains" (Ch.3)

"Blessed be happiness

Red Lake with Western Ghats in the background

the bubbling over happiness of little children" (Ch.4)

"A squirrel makes a charming pet"(ch.4)

"Watching birds build their nests and rear their young"

Playing at being lizards...

and here's the real lizard! (ch.5)

"Children are so forgiving" (ch.5)

"It was the young children's singing that drew me to want to hear the Gospel, and also their happiness" (ch.7)

"A green thought in a green shade" (Our Forest) (ch.10)

"A ravine carved out of a mighty forest" (Marahatha Pool)

"Our First House" (The Forest House)

The Jewel House

"We had found that boys often needed protection"

Being kind and gentle to animals

Learning to help one another

*(Both these pictures are of bygone days
developed from slides prepared nearly half a century back...)*

Two-way traffic!

Some of the daily chores

Fun in the Square

The old rocking horse

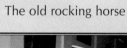

"We wanted to fill our children's mind

'Gold of dawn'

Some newly opened flowers to gaze at.

Heliconia

Gloriosa Lily

Water Lily

Some of our family cottages, seen from the House of Prayer tower

The Babies' Nursery

A cottage family

A new arrival

3 years later

Cottage prayer

Everyone needs attention!

Lunchtime

"Little Jeevalia girls in their nurseries learn how to help their Accals." (ch.13)

The Kindergarten

"A true teacher is a giver." (the Jeevalia School)

> **"Character is the thing we must make...**
> **but to attain it is not the work of a day and many must in**
> **truth lay down their lives if these things are to be."**

'I am sure no one can find
me here!'

'I've only
just learnt
to stand'

'Eat up, dolly'

'Peel this banana for me'

'We are friends'

'...and this is my friend.'

Days of youth:- growing, dreaming, having fun

'Timothys' — boarding school children

A game of 'Throw-ball'

Rehearsal for 'Family'
entertainment

Student nurses

Service to others never ends

Trained, experienced: God calls them back home to serve

Grannies love to help children as well as spoil them!

Present-giving on **Christmas Day**

Joy-bells

Pre-dawn carol singing on
Christmas morning

Singing round the Christmas Tree

Easter Day

Path of Quietness leading to God's Garden

Flowers under the Cross

Amma's Birthday Feast

The House of Prayer (ch.16)

Porana (ch.17)

"One of our nursery trellises is green with Porana all the year round"

Coming Day Room Decoration (ch.19)

"On Coming Days it was always Kohila's hands that made our rooms beautiful"

"She was very fond of growing plants"

The special purple flower that Kohila gathered for a friend's Coming-Day ...Love for others was her last thought"

'Our little house called 'Joppa' (by the sea) (ch.21)

Some of our Family on holiday at 'Joppa'

"Place of fresh winds and wide views" - Pavilions

The family gathering groundnuts

The Three-Pavilions' family

scraping sisal fibre

Articles made of sisal

Place of Healing - Parama Suha Salai (ch.25)

The Room of Vision above the operating theatre

"The colours of those working for the ill stand for integrity as well as love

"Serving our Lord in serving the ill"

Pharmacy

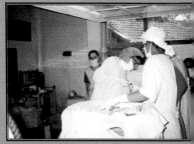

operating theatre

Place of Healing - Parama Suha Salai

"Reward for any kind of service never came into our scheme of things except the reward of giving pleasure or help"

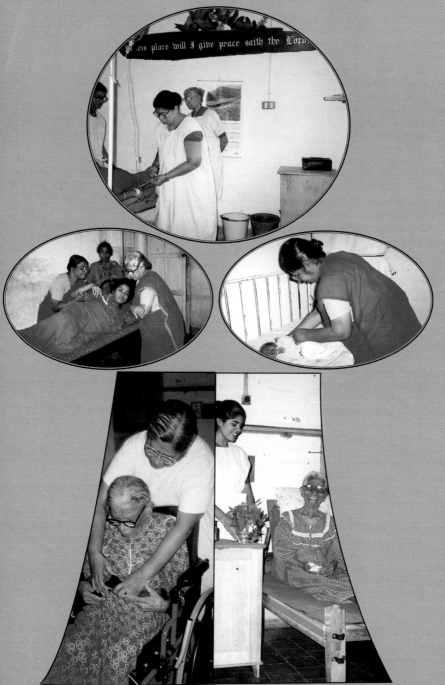

Place of Healing - Parama Suha Salai (ch.25)

Brothers and Sisters 'share their pot of honey'

Mimosa's grandson and great-grandson (ch.26)

'Won't you share your joke with us?'

Passion flower (ch.27)

Hall of Good Tidings (ch.33)

THE WHEEL

"THEY DWELT WITH

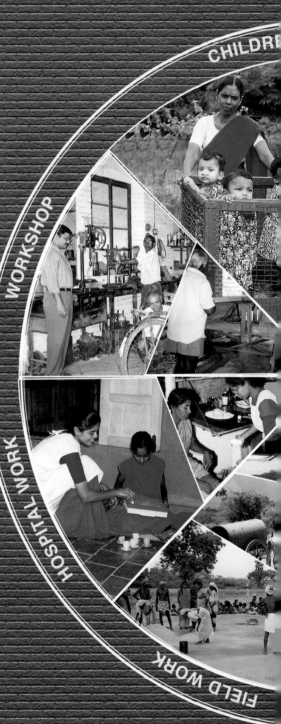

CHILDRE

WORKSHOP

HOSPITAL WORK

FIELD WORK

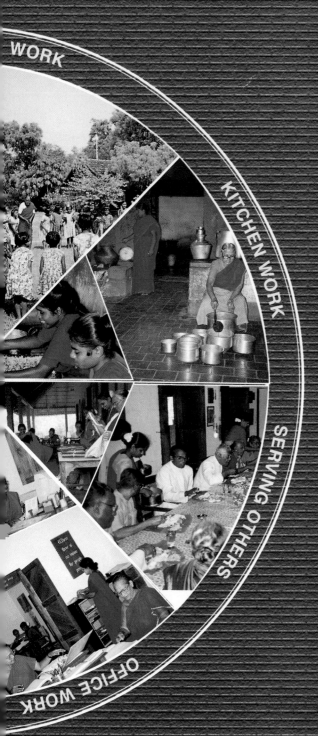

WORK

KITCHEN WORK

SERVING OTHERS

OFFICE WORK

PART 3

SOLDIERSHIP

He had realised long ago that the perfect journey is a perfect routine. Set a high standard, make a habit of it, and a good day's work is achieved with less physical or mental strain than if it is considered as a record.

Gino Watkins, by J.M. Scott.

Grant us inward fortitude;
Will to choose the highest good;
Eyes to see the jewel set
In plain duty's coronet.

Spirits sensitive and pure,
Disciplined to serve, endure;
And fulfilled with sweet content,
All their powers to please Thee bent.

There are ten strong things in the world, say the Rabbis: rock is strong but iron cleaves it; fire melts iron; water extinguishes fire; the clouds bear aloft the water; the wind drives away the clouds; man withstands the wind; fear unmans man; wine dispels fear; sleep overcomes wine; and death sweeps away even sleep. But strongest of all is lovingkindness, for it defies and survives death.

Dr. Hertz.

18. VOCATIONAL TRAINING*

And they fought with gladness the battle of Israel. I Mac.3.2.
My vocation is no game.

The Golden Road, Raymond De Perrot.

THERE came a day in Kohila's story when she heard the call of her Lord to offer herself to Him for His service. It was a happy day—as happy as the day when the Keeper of the Gate opened it to Christiana and called to the trumpeter that was above, over the Gate, to entertain Christiana with shouting and sound of trumpet for joy. So he obeyed, and sounded, and filled the air with his melodious notes.

And yet, to one looking on from outside and deaf to those melodious notes, all that would have been seen was the passing over of a school-girl to the nurseries, a very matter-of-fact affair about which no one made any fuss at all. But deep in her heart Kohila was happy, for she heard the melodious notes. She was going to be trained as a hospital nurse, and first would learn to help in the nurseries.

A sentence from I Chron. 26 shows how the day's work was regarded; it was simply "the business of the Lord and in the service of the King." For every matter pertaining to God and the affairs of the King we had the assurance of His help and continual presence. We took it for granted that His servant's one desire was to be spent out, with no reserves and no choices, to the uttermost in that service. For if children were to be saved from evil, many must be ready to count nothing secular, if only it helped towards their salvation.

---

* " 'Calling' and 'vocation' are Saxon and Latin words for the same thing, teaching us that God calls us to serve Him in any and every walk of life." Dictionary of Bible Phrases. W.K.Lowther Clarke, D.D.

83

Indeed, the words "secular and sacred" were never in our vocabulary as words of contrast. All was sacred. The things that some would call merely earthly, were not common things. They were pertaining to God; they were the business of the Lord, the affairs of the King. A Lotus bud senior to Kohila printed over the door of her new home when she was married to one like-minded: *Thy servants are ready to do whatsoever my Lord the King shall appoint,* and whatsoever meant *anything.*

So Kohila became a "Helping younger sister" to an older girl, and learned how to handle small children, remembering that each was a separate little person. And she scrubbed the tiled floors, drew water, washed the children's things and did all that in her lay to help the Accal in charge of the nursery. She found no difficulty here. Her pleasure "in keeping the backs of places nice" came into full play, and also her love of helping anyone and making everyone happy. As a nine-year-old school-girl she could be left by her Accal in charge of a roomful of small companions. The younger ones were sure to be good if Kohila was with them. So this part of her training ran smoothly.

Work in a nursery for children of the Buds' and Teddies' age followed, and here again all went well. A little kindergarten training was part of life now, and the necessary discipline, which included *thittum* (as the word sounds; it means precision), was sometimes a trial. But Kohila was naturally sensible and soon saw the point of the irritating demands of *thittum.* It was when she was given charge of a nursery with younger girls to train and to influence that the first difficulty appeared.

For as the testing stone is to the Indian goldsmith, so was this new responsibility to Kohila; if the gold be not quite pure, the stone shows the alloy. The alloy that was discovered in her gold was a weakness which leaned towards shielding a wrongdoer, or even sympathising with her, rather than taking the harder way of love without dissimulation, the noblest kind of help that soul can offer soul, and by far the most costly.

Once, and this was indeed a grievous time, a special friend of Kohila's caused a younger one to stumble by teaching her to deceive. Kohila's judgment was influenced by her fondness for her friend. She admitted the wrongdoing but condoned it. She did what Samuel refused to do for Saul. (Honour me now, I pray thee, before the elders of my people.) She forgot her Lord's solemn words about the millstone and the sea. Her sympathy was rather with the offender than with Him who was offended in the offence done to His little one.

But syrupy affection never yet led to spiritual integrity. And though it looks so like the charity which is greater than faith and hope that it is "admired of many," it is not admirable. It is sin.

And it is a blinding sin. It blinds the eyes to facts; and it leads to disaster, for it cuts the nerve of that happy confidence which is essential to spiritual co-operation. How could Kohila's fellow-workers feel sure of her if they could not count on her?

For the trustful must be able to trust that which is understood rather than stated in the commerce of common life, and take for granted without a flicker of doubt that which transcends the letter, because it is spirit, and spirit is pure truth. When he who called himself the Emperor of Cyprus surrendered to Richard Coeur de Lion he made one condition: he was not to be put in irons. "This condition Richard granted, and he strictly kept his word by loading the prisoner with chains that were made of silver." There are many ways by which one may "strictly keep" one's word and yet break it; for the finer shades of honour pass the confines of our speech.

The upright older girls, who, like the older boys and men and women whom we have now, require of themselves and demand of others the sword-blade quality of loyalty, were uneasy as they noticed this dust on Kohila's sword, this alloy in her gold. And her angel must have watched her with tender solicitude. Would she conquer, and become able for the hardest things, one whom a crisis finds unshakeable, or would she yield and miss the greatest opportunity that can be offered to any servant of the Lord? "Thy silver is become dross, thy wine is mixed with water," would it be that? Or would there be an honest recognition of the peril? Nothing less would lead her to her Lord who was waiting to turn His hand upon her, and throughly purge away her dross, and take away all her alloy.

But perhaps the angels see as their Lord does, when He calls the things that are not, as though they were (continually anticipating the birth of things that give as yet no token of existence *). If so, there must be always the rejoicing of hope, for they have had long experience of the power of His stern yet so compassionate love. And experience worketh hope.

"Failure is only fatal when it drives us in upon ourselves"; and failure drove Kohila to the Christ of Calvary who was even then saying to her, "Nothing can hurt thee but sin; nothing can grieve Me but sin; nothing can make thee base before thy foes but sin: Take heed of sin, My Mansoul," and this other word too, "Look therefore that thou wash often in My fountain, and go not in defiled garments."

Among our choruses is one which we usually sing as a prayer for wandering souls, but the "we" of the last line Kohila turned to "I," for she knew that she could not help another farther in the ways of God than she had gone herself. And so she prayed about that fatal tendency to be influenced by personal feelings:

---

* Rom. 4.17. Way.

Jesus, mighty Saviour,
Lover of the soul,
Who but Thee can quicken,
Who but Thee make whole?
This that I have brought Thee
Is too hard for me,
But is anything too hard, my Lord, for Thee?
By Thy Cross and Passion,
Precious Blood outpoured,
Plead I now, command deliverance, Blessed Lord.

But, like every child of the Father, she had to learn that the looking away from all that distracts on earth, ourselves especially, was not only a matter of the first moment of temptation, but must be the attitude of the soul. Looking away unto Jesus, "the word does not occur elsewhere in the New Testament or in the Septuagint," * and when a word occurs only once in the Scriptures, it is as if someone waved a flag before us, or sounded a blast on one of the silver trumpets of heaven—those trumpets that welcomes Christiana in at the gates. We cannot help seeing and hearing, and the word becomes alive to us for ever.

So Kohila passed through her testing time, "The devil is but God's Master-fencer to teach us to handle our weapons"; she was taught to handle her weapons. And, looking back upon her first two years of training, she remembered the happiness that spread like sunshine over the way, far more clearly than the shady patches that crossed it at times.

There were of course, days when things seemed to tumble one on top of the other, to the great discomfiture of her soul till she learned that things do not really behave in that way, though they

* *Westcott* on Hebrews 12.1.

sometimes seem to do so. Also she learned, and this was reassuring, that duties do not clash any more than do the stars. If we become inwardly rushed we shall feel as if they were all demanding attention at once. But if we are inwardly quiet we shall see the purposed sequence and take them one by one. An angel is never sent on more than one errand at a time, is the Jewish comment on the story of the three angels who appeared unto Abraham in the heat of the day. One came to foretell the birth of Isaac, one to speak of Sodom, one to rescue Lot. Our Father is as careful of us as He is of His angels.

These things Kohila learned, or at least began to learn, for to the end we are only learners. Above all, she learned to lean on the God of her Strength, the God of her joy and gladness. "Sing we merrily unto God our Strength"—the words ring like a chime of bells.

19. RATHER LIKE KING DAVID

(The Chief Shepherd to Sir Nameless, Guardian of the King's well:)
"I am the Chief Shepherd of the Valley of Toil, and I water my flocks by the King's Waters. And this thy charge is one of the noblest and most bountiful of the King's Wells...The King forgets none who are faithful, and has much love for those Nameless Knights who keep his lonely outposts, making beautiful many leagues of the Splendid Way and feeding many flocks by the fair waters of the King's bounty."

Sir Knight of the Splendid Way, by W.E. Cule.

WHEN Kohila was about twelve years old, one had joined our Fellowship who signed herself "Yours in His obedience." She was a nurse, and all her leanings were naturally towards nursing, but we had so very few teachers then that she turned to the place of greatest need, the Jeevalia, and helped to teach groups of children, of whom Kohila was one.

No one would ever have thought, as they saw her with a cluster of little girls round her, that this work was not the very choice of her heart. "She always seems to have that touch of genius that can make a party out of all she does. Do you know what I mean? a sort of perpetual Christmas-tree which she creates out of any work that comes her way," wrote her sister eighteen years afterwards. So Mary Mills made "a party" and a Christmas-tree out of her classes in the Jeevalia, and went on doing so till we had more help there.

But by the time Kohila was ready for hospital-training she was in her rightful place, and Kohila always looked to her as the one who taught her what it means to serve our Lord in serving the ill: "I was sick and ye visited Me."

And when May Powell, our Doctor Sittie, came (her Tamil

name means Aid in time of need), Kohila and all the girls then
beginning their training found her just what they had found their
other Sitties to be: *sonthum* (own, heart's own) one to be counted
on without fear of ever being disappointed in their trust.

We had at that time only two small wards, gift of friends in
the United States, and called Hope. One of our first patients was a
widow who was crushed and bruised and broken, and she received
hope, for the God of Hope became her Saviour and Lord. Her
town is wholly Hindu, and she was the first from that town to turn
to the living God. After a while a Scotsman gave us a little hospital
for our small children. It was called Others because it was given in
memory of his mother, "who always thought of others." And
Kohila, who received most of her training there, took its name as a
motto for her life.

"When we had sick babies," writes one of the nursery
nurses, "we were always at rest about them when Kohila had them;
she never thought of herself, only of others. It was always Christ,
others, Kohila. Never was she anywhere but third.

"Sometimes a difficult girl came to be trained. Kohila
always made that girl her friend and all her influence was
used to help her to be kind and good, and if she was quarrelsome
she tried to make her peaceful. She had one weakness. She still
found it hard to stand bravely for the right, because if she did so,
she knew it would hurt and perhaps offend the one who was wrong.
But this weakness she had most earnestly set herself to overcome.

"Sometimes her memory was a difficulty. She would get
things mixed in her mind, and she never could explain properly
how it happened; but she used to go away and pray about the
matter, and then go and work hard in the garden, and that helped
her."

Often we have noticed that gardens help; the very feel of the earth seems to help, and the touch of leaves and flowers. Perhaps what they do for us is a legacy from Eden. However it be, it is often true that an hour among green things "changes the face of the matter," as the garrulous woman of Tekoa said about something else. And when it leads to the giving of much pleasure to your friends, then naturally even digging is a healing occupation. "She was very fond of growing plants, so that she might have flowers to give to us all, and on the Coming-days it was always Kohila's hands that made our rooms beautiful," is the word of her fellow-nurses.

Another friend brings this, a night-duty memory. "She did not like night-duty; but, *Bless ye the Lord, all ye servants of the Lord, which by night stand in the house of the Lord*, helped her very much." She often sang Mary Dobson's song,

There is a King who cometh in the morning;
    If that He find thee working in the garden,
Thou art His son.

There is a King who cometh in the noontide;
    If that He find thee praying at His footstool,
He heareth thee.

There is a King who cometh in the gloaming;
    If that He find thee watching by some sufferer,
He crowneth thee.

The Tamils make much of friendship. If there be no affinity of spirit, they say that though one live with another for a long time, if parted, the friendship quickly dissolves; but is it possible to let go attachment's well-knit ties, though those to whom one's soul be knit dwell many days afar? And again, The use and wont of friendship is that, what once it has loved, it loves always. It is likened to the flower on the flowering tree. When the flower has blossomed it remains in bloom till the petals fall—this in contrast to the lotus, which opens and closes again. And a favourite comparison is that of the goldsmith's pincers, which drop the gold put into the crucible, whereas his rod enters the fire with the gold. He is a friend who stands by us in joy and in sorrow, in hunger, in affliction from enemies, at the door of the prince, and in the burning-ground.*

All this is in the fibre of these people. One can appeal to it and be sure of response.

Kohila was a loyal friend. "She had such a deep love 0for everybody that I cannot remember her not loving anybody," writes the girl who was with her when she set out on her last walk up the mountain to gather a special purple flower for a friend's Coming-day. "She never thought of putting herself first in any way. And everybody in trouble went to her. She was rather like King David when he was in the cave, and everyone that was in distress and discontented gathered themselves unto him; for all who were like that went to her, and some became good through her influence."

When babies died, and their special Accals felt as anyone who has loved and nursed a baby and seen it die cannot help feeling, however sure the certainty be that the little one is safe and well and good and happy for ever, Kohila comforted them very tenderly. Once, when one of the Accals had this sweet sorrow (sweet, because sinless), Kohila went to her, *"For a little while,"* she said, and the words come back to us now; we have parted, but only "for a little while."

When first we began to save babies, we could not persuade any of the village mothers to help us with the more delicate, but by

---

* From the Tamil Classic *Naladiyar* translated by Dr. Pope of Oxford.

the time Kohila was a nurse there were between twenty and thirty who were ready to be foster-mothers, and among these women, some nominal Christians, some Hindus, Kohila found her mission-field. The women grew to love her, and gave her a name meaning the Meritorious one—merit is a great word in India, though they all knew that no thought of merit entered into her mind. It was the overflow that could not help overflowing:

> *"Thou be my loving that I Thy love sing,"* *
> *Thou be my longing that I to Thee cling,*
> *Thou be my thinking that I Thy will know,*
> *Thou be my willing that I Thy will do,*
> *Me to redeem, Thou didst die on the Tree;*
> *Dearworthy, dearworthy art Thou to me.*

That was how it was. How, then, endure the thought, how become accustomed to it, that He was not dear to others too?

---

* Richard Rolle, fourteenth century.

20. CLIMBING

Man's supreme adventure in the material world was seen to be symbolical of supreme adventure in the realm of the spirit. And this record of the Everest climbers' undaunted efforts has come to be an inspiration not only to mountaineers and geographers, but also to that far more numerous host of humble yet ambitious strivers after the topmost pinnacle of achievement in the varied branches of human activity.

From the Foreword of *Everest* 1933, Hugh Ruttledge.

O Thou to whom man's heart is known,
Grant me my morning orison...
May I ne'er lag, nor hapless fall,
Nor weary at the battle-call!

The Moon Endureth, John Buchan.

THE Life of Dr. Randall Davidson, Archbishop of Canterbury, is not a book that came into Kohila's hands. It would have been too far out of her world to do much for her. And she could not have had any idea of what the pressure on his life was. (And yet he could make time to care for and inquire about a battle that filled our days when she was a child and helped to build the Jewel House.) But if she had read that book she would have marked, and, according to her custom, passed on these words of his: *Grant, O Lord, that in the weariness of unceasing work our intercourse with Thee may ever be fresh.*

For though she was only a little Indian nurse, life was not an easy way for her. At times there was the reproach of the Cross, and "No man hath a velvet Cross." It was also always a climb.

"I was not worthy of her friendship," writes a fellow-nurse, "for I never rose to the place where she was, but she was constantly helping me to rise." This was a hidden ministry, as hidden as the bird whose song you hear as you pass through a wood—you do not always see the singer. Sheaves of notes in Tamil and English have been kept and treasured by her fellow-workers, whom she dearly loved with the love that was God's gift to her. For one who was tempted to be satisfied with the ordinary, cool and measured love so many offer to the Lord, she printed in blue on a strip of paper the well-known words: "Jesus will be loved alone above all things. Let Jesus alone be specially beloved."

Among these treasured things is a strip of ribbon. Jeevanie, one of Kohila's fellow-nurses, was not strong, and for a nurse to be ailing is not easy. Someone gave Kohila that morsel of ribbon, and she painted on it *His loving arms shall bear thee all the day.* And again (this was in Tamil), *Thou shalt know hereafter.*

The day came when that nurse, now recovered, gave her marked New Testament to a poor village woman who was slowly dying in pain and tempted to feel forsaken. "She has a Bible, but the print is small, and my New Testament has large print, so I want her to have it," said Jeevanie in speaking of this. "And see, I have pasted Kohila's words in it for her." There is something as imperishable in the seed of love as in the seed of song. Could there be a more fruitful work than the training of sowers to sow that seed?

But I cannot wonder when any of our children become what true lovers should be. They see before them night and day that which we hope they will be. Soon after Kohila went into training, a baby boy was very ill, and for several days was allowed no food except water. Every Indian knows, of course, that to give mere water is fatal, and every one was sure that he would die. One night, being very anxious, I went to see the baby. It was long after midnight, but I saw kneeling on either side of his cot the doctor who at that time was our guest, but who was afterwards to become our own, and the Beloved Sittie.

The baby recovered, and a photo taken soon afterwards shows him more smile than baby; for he poked his head out of his swinging hammock and almost all that could be seen of him was one immense smile.

There are many memories of those days. One of them carries our thoughts back to a time when a little five-year-old Kohila was all but caught by the vehemence of the storm against the wall.

Along the front of the babies' hospital there are low steps, and when no one was very ill and there was a little free time in the evenings, their Sittie would gather the young nurses together and they would sit on those steps and sing. She taught them to sing in parts— something they greatly enjoy—and on an evening when they longed to bring comfort to one whom they loved, they slipped away quietly, and suddenly through the stillness of the room rang the sweet, silver notes of a chant: *For Thou hast been a strength to the poor, a strength to the needy in his distress, a refuge from the storm, a shadow from the heat, when the blast of the terrible ones is as a storm against the wall.*

Thank God, thank God for those young lives not needy, not distressed, not out in the storm, not out in the heat, but for ever safe from the blast of the terrible ones when it is as a storm against the wall.

Once, after Kohila had become Head Nurse, something went wrong, and the Sittie, Margaret Sutherland, who was then in charge of the nurses-in-training, and whose Tamil name means Patience, thought that a talk might help. It was after what we call in our human speech an accident had occurred that kept me in bonds, so that the family came to me; I could not go to them. I tell the very little tale because it shows, as no other I can gather does, a certain sturdiness that was Kohila's.

We had talked over the difficulty and had found a place of peace, when suddenly Kohila, who, like the other nurses, was sitting on the floor close by me, sprang up. "*Don't* think, Amma," she said earnestly, "that anything will ever make us want to part with our dear Patience Sittie!" Her loyal soul had suddenly feared lest the difficulty should in any way reflect on that Sittie (it did not do so at all). "Patience is her name and Patience is her character," she said, as she sat down, reassured.

After Kohila's swift passing, Patience wrote to me, "Love for others was her last thought. If there was a difficult case it was always Kohila who took it on, or a difficult nurse it was always Kohila who offered to work with her; if someone was needed to *buthil* it was always Kohila who volunteered to miss the treat." It was the word of all others, which Patience knew would make me glad, for it is in the common ways of unselfishness that the lovers of our Lord show the love that He is perfecting in them.

And He was perfecting truth in the recesses of the heart, the inward parts. Her Annãchie remembers a note he received one day from Kohila. From time to time he gathered stories of worth, had them typed and sent them round the family. Each one ticked his or her name off the list as the typescript was received, read and passed on. A busy nurse may not always have time to read and, probably without thinking of what it implied, Kohila sometimes ticked her name off the list, and passed the story on without having read it.

And then one day she saw this tick on the envelope as untruth, and she wrote at once to her Annãchie and told him about those ticks.

When I heard of it I remembered how, when I first saw the "Not-at-home boxes" which are hung upon the gates of Indian bungalows, though very likely their owners are at home, someone explained, "Oh, it's only a polite fiction, like 'I am so glad to see you,' and 'I regret to refuse.'" But Kohila knew nothing of polite fictions.

Nor did she know anything of those comfortable excuses we so easily make for ourselves. She had been trained in spiritual honesty, and she knew well that anything approaching insincerity was sin, and remembering her early weakness along this line, she feared to be ensnared again. *In No Cross no Crown* there are straight words about that which causes one to yield to a besetting sin: "I lay this down as the undoubted reason of this degeneracy, to wit, the inward disregard of thy mind to the light of Christ shining in thee, that first showed thee thy sins and reproved thee, and that taught and enabled thee to deny and resist them. So when thou didst begin to disregard that light and grace, to be careless of that holy watch that was once set up in thine heart, and didst not keep sentinel there, as formerly, for God's glory and thine own peace, the restless enemy of man's good quickly took advantage of this slackness, and often surprised thee with temptations, whose suitableness to thy inclinations made his conquest over thee not difficult."

Parts of this old book, whose title is known better than its contents, helped to form Kohila.

21. UNIMPEDED COMMERCE WITH THE SUN

I must wait betimes at His gate,
Ere the hush of the dawn be broken,
Ere the hurry of life begin,
And the calm of the morn depart.
Some word for me alone
In the quietness may be spoken,
Which all through the live-long day
I shall carry deep in my heart.
From My Mother's Bible

WHEN Livingstone wrote his *Travels*, he spoke of certain trials inseparable from his life, but he added, "I do not mention these privations as if I considered them to be sacrifices, for I think that the word ought never to be applied to anything we can do for Him who came down from heaven and died for us." And he was right.

It is not sacrifice, it is joy to give ourselves wholly to our children and to the needy people about us. But breathing-spaces are required, and for the Indian, as much as for the foreign workers, times when, like the mountains, "we may grow more bright from unimpeded commerce with the sun." Our little house called Joppa (by the sea), the Forest, and Pavilions, which is just over the border of Travancore, gave this unimpeded commerce to Kohila. The Sittie in charge of Pavilions sees that the house we call Rest is restful for those who stay there. In all the little ways that make such a difference, she does as the keeper of the inn on the way to Jericho was told to do a long time ago—she "takes care" of them.

To this place of fresh winds and wide views Kohila and her fellow-nurses went after a time in the nurseries and hospital. And

101

when she returned after even only a fortnight away from home, we were always reminded of that rapturous moment, years ago, at the hot, crowded station of Erode, when the friends who had sheltered her brought her to meet us, and she sprang with one leap into the arms that were so glad to feel her there again, and with all four limbs hugged every inch of us that she could reach.

What is the chief blessing of Pavilions? We have asked more than one; nearly always the answer has been, "Time to be quiet." There is a cave in the rocks, and there are nooks among the boulders from which you can see the blue of the Indian Ocean and the great, encircling mountains. And though there are children at Pavilions— for it is one of our outposts—the responsibility of their affairs is not upon the visitor. She can be quiet for as long as she wishes.

And there are books, as at all our various houses; and sometimes a girl tempted to what we call "a mushy friendship" has been helped out of that quagmire by reading such words as these of Oswald Chambers', which exactly meet a condition not unknown in India and perhaps elsewhere:

"What has been like water from the well of Bethlehem to you recently? Love, friendship, spiritual blessing? Then at the peril of your soul you take it to satisfy yourself. If you do, you cannot pour out before the Lord. How am I to pour out spiritual gifts, or natural friendship or love? How can I give them to the Lord? In one way only—in the determination of my mind, and that takes about two seconds. If I hold spiritual blessings or friendships for myself they will corrupt me, no matter how beautiful they are. I have to pour them out before the Lord, give them to Him in my mind, though it looks as if I am wasting them; even as when David poured the water out on the sand, to be instantly sucked up."

How very little, we have often found ourselves thinking as we took a visitor round nurseries, schoolrooms, playgrounds, hospital, or even out to the villages where much of our work directly and indirectlylies—how very little is ever seen of what really is. We pass a girl who looks up from her work and smiles, "What a happy face ! " says the guest. We pass a rampageous bunch of boys, "I have never seen happier lads." And yet all the time a relentless war is being waged against forces incalculable in subtlety and strength. We are continually looking at invisible battle-fields. That girl who smiled so cheerily is going through a test of fortitude and constancy, which, could she know it, would send the visitor speechless to her knees. One of those merry boys lately fought, and by God's grace won, in a conflict of which none caught the slightest glimpse but those who had his deepest confidence. And it is so everywhere. Not one is overlooked by the enemy unless he slip out of the firing-line. When that happens there may be a great calm—but it is the calm of death.

Thank God, many are learning to use the very winds that seek to uproot them, as the pilot of the sailplane (taught by the birds) uses the winds and the currents of the air. But the soul sometimes tires, even as it rises. Effortless ease and spiritual uprising and the lifting of others do not run together, ever.

At one time some of the thoughts which were trying to disturb the peace of faithful workers were put into words thus :

His thoughts said, When I would seek Him whom my soul loveth, confusions like flies buzz about me.

His Father said, Press through these confusions as thou wouldest press through a swarm of gnats. Take no notice of them. Be not stayed by them. Be not occupied with them.

His thoughts said, It is too much to hope that such a one as I am should truly please my Lord.

His Father said, But it is written, It is God which worketh in you both to will and to do of His good pleasure. In My servant Paul I wrought an earnest expectation and a hope that in nothing he should be ashamed, but that always Christ should be magnified in his body. I am the God of thine expectation and thy hope.

His thoughts said, But I am not St. Paul.

His Father said, Hast thou watched a wave fill a shell on the shore? Thou art My shell. I am the God of thy hope. Wave upon wave I will flow over thee, poor empty shell that thou art. With all joy and peace I will fill thee, and thou shalt abound in hope.

His thoughts said, What of those whom I love and long to help but cannot?

His Father said, Am I a God at hand, and not a God afar off? Am I not with them, My child? Thou knowest that I am.

His thoughts said, But it is hard not to be with them, especially in their hours of sorrow and of joy.

His Father said, When such desires cannot be granted, think of My two angels on the day of thy Saviour's ascension. In that great hour of His joy, as He was welcomed Home, they were not there with Him. I could trust them willingly to do My will elsewhere. Let it be so with thee.

Was it "chance" that caused the 94th Psalm to be appointed for the fourth day of the week—our Wednesday? The beginning of anything is cool and dewy, the light of dawn is on it. The ending has its private charm. But the middle? Mid-day, the hot mid-day of the week, middle-life, when the throng of things presses—these middles of things can find us in the place where we understand the beautiful old Septuagint word "soothed." *When my distracted thoughts crowd within me* (as one rendering of Ps. 94.19 has it), *Thy consolations have soothed my soul*: "A dew coming after heat refresheth."

How often we have been tempted to wish that we could shelter one and another, Indian and foreign too, from hurting things, especially from the long ache of battle wounds. Vain wish and foolish.

We never can. We can only watch, as perhaps their angels watch while they go through everything, more than conquerors by the grace of the Conqueror.

His thoughts said, I cannot go on any longer.

His Father said, Thou canst. Thou canst do all things I appoint, through Christ which strengtheneth thee. Doth the burning sun distress thee? There shall be a shadow from the heat. Art thou beaten by the storm? There shall be a covert for thee from storm and from rain. Dost thou say with another servant of Mine, "My daily furnace is the tongue of men"? Thou knowest how to find thy way to the Pavilion, where thou shalt be kept from the strife of tongues. Or is it that thou art too weary to know why thou art so weary? Then come unto Me and I will refresh thee,

Heart that is weary because of the way,
Facing the wind and the sting of the spray,
Come unto Me, and I will refresh you.

Heart that has tasted of travail and toil,
Burdened for souls whom the foe would despoil,
Come unto Me, and I will refresh you.

Heart that is frozen—a handful of snow,
Heart that is faded—a sky without glow,
Come unto Me, and I will refresh you.

Heart that is weary, O come unto Me.
Fear not, whatever the trouble may be,
Come unto Me, and I will refresh you.

In many of Kohila's notes to her girl-friends she wrote of what a difference it made if one had Quiet in the early morning. She had found that she could not live without it. One of them once wrote something she had come across in a book, and hung it up in the kitchen, "Beware of saying I have no time to read my Bible and pray; but rather say, I have not bothered to discipline myself to do those things." But this self-discipline meant rising at half-past five or earlier, and we are glad when the laborious work which long ago we taught our family to welcome, not to hate, can cease for a while, and we can send the worker away to a place where she can sleep as long as she likes and yet have uninterrupted time afterwards. Kohila and others found it "soothing," like the consolations of the Lord. And she found it good to dwell in the help of the Highest, to sojourn under the shadow of the God of heaven, to say to Him, "Thou art my Helper and my Refuge; my God, I will hope in Thee", and to receive in peacefulness the inward assurance that He would "deliver her from every troublesome matter,"* even the troublesome matter that perhaps had tried to chase after her to Pavilions and rob her of her peace.

A sentence from one of my mother's letters helped many a young worker beset as all are, if indeed they are taking up their Cross daily and following their Lord. "The devil can wall us in, but he cannot roof us over. We can always get out at the top. Our difficulties are God's challenges, and He lets them be so hard often, that we must either go under or rise above them. Such an hour brings out the highest possibilities of faith, and we are pushed by the very emergency into God's best."

---

* Ps. 91.4, LXX.

22. FALLINGS FROM US, VANISHINGS

He had spoken of sufferings inflicted by the world. But this was not all. There are trials within—"fallings from us, vanishings"—swhich are harder to endure than outward persecution. These also the apostles had to overcome.

Peterborough Sermons, Westcott.

Art thou disappointed? Come to Me;
I will never be a grief to thee.

Hurt by hand thou trusted? Come to Me;
Leaves of healing I will lay on thee.

Art thou broken? Come, My child, to Me;
I, thy Comforter, will comfort thee.

Even friends can sometimes changeful be;
I will always be the same to thee.

IT is difficult to look back over any story which tells of the lovingkindness of the Lord, without giving an impression which is untrue. I have often watched in wonder the lovely lightness of a little bird who seems to think himself from bough to bough. He is here one moment, and the next, there. You hardly see his flight: it is something between flesh and spirit in its ease and swift sureness. A truer picture of our life is the mountaineer's climb, often so slow that we do not seem to be climbing at all.

There were griefs which shadowed us at times, till we could hardly see the blue in the sky above us, although there was always far more blue than grey.

One of these griefs closely touched Kohila, and tried her and perplexed her, for the one concerned was her own Accal. We were so short-handed when she was a little girl that a fellow- missionary, wanting

107

to help us, sent us a girl who was, she believed, fit to train young children. Kohila was one of the group of children in her charge, and to the lack of the finer sense of honour which we did not discover till the older girl had been with us for some years, we attribute much of Kohila's difficulty in attaining to flawless truth. For we have proved again and again that as the Accal of a nursery is, so are the children. They reflect her as water reflects its surroundings.

When at last we knew that this girl whom we had trusted could not be depended on for what we most earnestly desired, and when all we could do to help her was resented as "lack of love," when we saw that it was not in her to teach our children to whip hypocrisy off the field of life, then we knew that we could not go on. There were places elsewhere ready to welcome her, and she has done well—as the world counts well—but as a spiritual trainer of children, as we understand the word, she was impossible. So she went out from us, but she was not of us, for if she had been of us she would no doubt have continued with us.

This was Kohila's first great trouble. It was one that we, to whom the larger responsibilites of the work were committed, were to have more than once; and each such experience stands out in memory as a walk through The Pass of Tears.

The name comes from the very beautiful story, *Sir Knight of the Splendid Way*. One who has been overcome says sadly, "This pass is a Pass Perilous in which the bravest heart may fight in vain. It is strewn with broken blades and rusted armour." The holders of the Pass are two Veiled Sisters (veiled because of the mystery which enshrouds them) who sometimes go together and sometimes go alone, "but both have might and power, whether together or apart," and yet, the story tells us, it is commanded that if any in the Pass speak to them in the King's Name, they must lead him to the presence of the Warden of the Pass. *"For in the King's power I have conquered them"* (says the Warden), *"and they must obey."*

So as we, like others, had to walk in this Pass, there were sorrows, "fallings from us, vanishings," whose painfulness only the loving heart can ever comprehend; words like those in I John 2. 19 explain them, but they cannot comfort them.

And there were illnesses, for Kohila was not very strong. But "God help us if we are not better than our bodies' inclinations"; the spirit of man will sustain his infirmity, is a great word for the ill, if only by the grace of the Lord, the Conqueror of pain, they can lay hold upon it. And Kohila did. Her fellow-nurses say of her, "She was not an ordinary patient. She never forgot that she was a nurse, and so must be a perfect patient." From time to time also there were the trials and tests that must be if life is to be more than a painted pretence. Each one of these had a share in shaping the child of this story. We thought of everything as preparation for service, witness-bearing and soul-winning in the Place of Healing and the villages. But now we know that it was preparation for another Service, Elsewhere.

23. "LIVE LOOSE TO THEM"

You ask, how long the strife shall last?
It lasts till all your life is past;
Till, breaking peace with Compromise,
To sacrificial heights you rise,
Until your will no more is weak,
And all your coward doubtings fall
Before the message, Naught or All.
And what the loss? Your idols broken,
Your faint-heart feastday-keeping gone,
Each golden chain, Your slavery's token,
All that your slackness slumbers on,
And what the prize? A will new-born,
A soul at one, a faith with wings;
A sacrificial joy, that flings
Even to the grave nor yet complains;
On each man's brow a crown of thorn;
Yes, these shall be your victory's gains.

Brand, Henrik Ibsen.

Practically everything of real value to them was burnt. Later, Goforth tried to comfort his wife by saying, "My dear, do not grieve so. After all, they're *just things.*"

Goforth of China, Rosalind Goforth.

AMONG our customs is one which has been a blessing to many. Each child has what is called a Pon Accal. Pon is one of the many words which means Gold. Golden older sister is the older one's name henceforth, and to her the younger one is Golden little sister. The Pon Accal has a certain responsibility towards her younger sister, and very faithfully fulfils it.

Vineetha, one of the first generation of Lotus Buds, was Pon Accal to the nurses-in-training, and for some time she was troubled because Kohila clung to her own small room as a cat clings to its home. It had been hers ever since she began her training; her Beloved Sittie had given it to her. She could not give it up, even though she knew that it was needed now for another nurse.

"God often touches our best comforts that we may live loose to them. It was the doctrine of Jesus, that if thy right hand offend thee, thou must cut it off; and if thy right eye offend thee, thou must pluck it out; that is, if the most dear, the most useful and tender comforts thou enjoyest, stand in thy soul's way, *and interrupt thy obedience to the voice of God, and thy conformity to his holy will revealed in thy soul, thou art engaged, under the penalty of damnation, to part with them."*

This may sound harsh; but the Bible is not made of pleasing sentences. The words which William Law quoted are only a few grains from a great heap of grain—the grain of stern truth. But "Who can teach me, save He that enlighteneth my heart, and discovereth its dark corners?" The discovering light had not wrought yet in Kohila. She did not live loose to her room.

In a case like this you who are responsible to God for such a soul stand for a moment at the parting of the ways. You may say, "I wish the thing to be done," and it will be done. There is no travail if you take that way; but it leads nowhere. It never leads to spiritual victory farther on. Or you may put the responsibility for decision upon the one concerned, and then you will travail indeed. But in the end, if your hands be steady until the going down of the sun, eternal gain will be the outcome of that prayer and that travail.

At such times silence for a while is often best. Vineetha and others who knew about the matter said little, but they prayed much. And soon Kohila wrote a note to her Accal (it is always easier to write than to speak); she was very unhappy about not being willing to change her room, and yet she could not bear to think of leaving it. She told the exact and humiliating truth.

So Vineetha went to see her, and in her quiet, straight way she gave her younger sister the word of the Lord, that word whose entrance giveth light : gives it at once; pours it down, as often we see a sudden pouring down of light, almost like a waterfall of light through a little gap in our western hills. *Every one that hath forsaken houses for My Name's sake shall receive an hundred-fold,* was the word that she read then, the word that turned to light; and she told Kohila that here was her opportunity to help the younger girls to understand that self-discipline must underlie soul-winning. And instantly Kohila saw it. There might be clouds of feelings round about, but the light had found her.

After Vineetha left her, Kohila went to her cherished little room for a minute alone—one last precious minute. Then she went straight to the girl for whom the room was required, to whom she had spoken ungraciously, and she asked her pardon and "willingly with joy I give you my room," she said.

"And indeed she gave it with joy," says the girl who was to use it. "I never saw anything but joy on her face as she left it. There was no hesitation, only joy."

It must seem a little thing to Kohila now, if indeed she remembers it at all. "I go to prepare a place for you. And if I go and prepare a place for you, I will come again and receive you unto Myself; that where I am, there ye may be also." Lay those words alongside that clinging to earth which would hold one back from the highest, and the things of earth will fade even now while we are in the midst of them. How much more when we see the place that He went away to prepare for us? How much more when we see His face?

24. SELF-DISCIPLINE, SELF-PITY

Every moment of your lives you are exerting a tremendous influence, that will tell on the immortal interests of souls around you. Are you asleep, while your conduct is exerting such an influence?

Charles Finney.

He that is truly dedicate to war
Hath no self-love; nor he that loves himself
Hath not essentially, but by circumstance,
The name of valour.

Henry VI.

He had his task which must be done without thought of the price. The mainspring of his life was the Stoic precept: "We also must be soldiers, and in a campaign where there is no intermission and no discharge."

Augustus, John Buchan.

SELF-DISCIPLINE, soul-winning—these are two of the great words of life, and the sworn foe of both is self-pity. All the influences which surrounded this little nurse who was also to be God's warrior, were either guiding lights or beacons of warning; so part of the shaping was being done (quite unknown to themselves) by those who joined our Fellowship after she grew up. Some of these—the same is probably true elsewhere—had a high regard for the second of those two words, but hardly understood the alphabet of the first.

And yet it is *that*, or the absence thereof, that is observed long before the missionary can speak the language; and sometimes perhaps before the welcoming eyes of older ones see it, an inconspicuous Indian sister or brother has observed those unconscious gestures of the spirit that say so much more than words. There is no speech nor language where those voices are not heard.

Nothing on the part of the observer will betray this

115

scrutiny. But "I saw the Lord Jesus looking through his eyes," will be said of one who never for a moment imagined that he was all day long reminding people of his Lord; or, "Just to see her passing makes me want to be good," will be said (and both these words have been said) of one who could not speak Tamil.

It is the quality of the life that tells, and wins a loyalty that is imperishable as gold. It is not what is said that counts, but what *is*.

But possibly it may be otherwise. Not unkindly, but keenly, dark eyes are watching; if they see a girl, who is accustomed to being made much of, opening her ear to the whispered, "Pity thyself," confidence, if it has been given at all, is very quietly withdrawn. It is as if doors were softly shut. Then that unhappy one, remembering how much she was appreciated at home, feels sadly out of her element and wishes herself home again.

The same exactly applies to a man. Only he is probably less aware than the woman of the shut doors. He is cordial and kind to everyone. At home he was rather a special person. Unconsciously he takes it for granted that he is that here, or would be if only he had a fair chance. But deep within him the whisper has been admitted, not repulsed, "Pity thyself." He magnifies his difficulties, and probably puts them into an interesting article for a missionary magazine. And the magazine swallows it eagerly.

Little is seen by such a one of all that fellow-missionaries are trying to do to smooth the path and to surround with careful thoughtfulness every step of the way. Little is understood of the love that is flowing round him all the time. Nothing is felt but that "it is all so difficult." Seniors, if they do indeed love, make tender excuses, and they wait in quenchless hope; for in them is a longing that the new recruit will never know till he, if the Lord tarries, reaches the place where all has been poured out; and the heart's deepest prayer is for comrades with the strength and the fresh vision of youth (and also steadfastness) to carry on.

It is adulation that feeds self-pity. That vice fattens on the praise of man. Is he upon whom you like to lard the sweet sauce of spiritual flattery preparing to serve his Master in places where the fight is fierce? If so, I earnestly ask you to pause. Believe it— for it is true—you are making it much more difficult than God means it to be, for the one whom you admire to go through "the mill". And you are paving the way for disappointment for those to whom he goes.

The unfussed-over quietly pass through their first year without even knowing that it is a "mill". They are like sunshine and fresh wind to all about them. They cannot come into a room without refreshing somebody. The fussed-over is depressed, and depressing, and very hard to comfort; for by the time you have dealt with one grievance, another crops up. And the Indian (I write only of India) is helped or hindered by the one who is sent out as example and leader, just in proportion to the absence or presence of the many-coloured vice of self-pity.

But we have a merciful Lord; let any who are humble enough to recognise themselves as belonging by nature to the Order of the Self-Pitying, take heart. I have seen some pass through that dolorous experience and come out on the other side.

After all, why should one be sorry for oneself? What soldier ever asked for conflict without wounds? What climber prayed that he might reach the summit without fatigue? As for the insidious, "But I have no opportunity to speak a word for my Lord," it is the devil's masterstroke. The most persuasive Gospel message I have heard, and I must have heard thousands, was given by one who at that time hardly knew the difference between a Tamil verb and noun; and I have seen influences that I believe will have eternal results flow not from something said, but from

something done by one who was new to India and little dreamed
of the word that passed from mouth to mouth that day, *which is
the greater, to talk or to live?*

25. PREPARING FOR THE PLACE OF HEALING

An officer must be capable of understanding and combining in order to obey.
The Principles of War, Marshal Foch.

O my God, since Thou art with me, and I must now, in obedience to Thy commands, apply my mind to these outward things, I beseech Thee to grant me the grace to continue in Thy presence; and to this end do Thou prosper me with Thy assistance, receive all my works, and possess all my affections.
The Practice of the Presence of God.

IN that parable of life, the Song of Songs, we see the first work given to us to do under the figure of a garden enclosed, a spring shut up, a fountain sealed. We see our home as a place where souls learn to be indeed as gardens enclosed, shut up and sealed for their Owner. But it is more: it is a training-ground for souls. Every nursery, every schoolroom, every workshop, we see as that; and always in our thoughts and in our prayers we go on to the fountain of gardens, the well of living waters and streams from Lebanon—something for the good of others, the salvation of others, and their eternal refreshment.

Festival work and village preaching naturally offered opportunity. We opened several village outposts, and our workers lived happily among the people. But always a conversion or the sign of conversion meant that the people who wished to hear, dare not listen, because of their *gurus*, if they were Hindus, and their *mullahs* if they were Muslims; and at last we saw that our Father had some better thing for us—better, I mean, in that it would give us many more chances to preach the Gospel to the people of the very orthodox villages and towns. And so it came to pass that a Place of Healing was planned, a place where not only the ill would be welcomed, but also their relations and friends. Before it was possible to get such a place built, the Lord set His seal upon the thought by winning to Himself, in a little Indian house used till the larger place was ready, the first true convert from Islam any of us had ever seen or heard of in this part of Southern India.

His wife had heard the Gospel from one of us who was visiting his town, and she asked him, "Is it a true word—this of a Saviour who loves us and can save us from our sins?" He was an honest man, and in order to be able to answer her questions, he felt he must read our Book as well as his Koran. So he read the New Testament. But he could not believe it to be true, "because he had never seen the life lived that was spoken of in that Book." Then he brought a patient here, and as he watched day by day he "saw something of that life." This led to his conversion, and his wife and children joined him.

So with the thought not only of patients, but of their families as an evangelistic opportunity, medical work was carried on in a little house we called the The Door of Health. Hospital, a word most uncomfortably mispronounced in India, has two connotations here: one of help, one of dread. So we avoided it. And when a Hindu with an Indian's quick perceptions said of the first new building, "It will be a place of Other-world (Spiritual) healing" (for he knew that though all that could be done for the patients' help would be done, prayer and spiritual healing would be first with doctors and nurses), we took that word for its name, and at once it was adopted everywhere.

But I had hardly realised how much the name was to mean till a note came from a young Sittie who had been there. "I do wish that you could know the joy of this place. It's rather like His peace, because it passes understanding. Can you picture a Place of Healing where all the time one is surrounded by those who have in a mysterious way become 'own', and where there is complete confidence, and, above all, the joy and presence of our Lord? The fear of 'hospital' is just the fear of the very opposite to what is here. Thank you for giving it another name. Such a lovely word came this morning," (the morning before she was to go for treatment. It was the word, though she did not know it, that had been the doctor's years ago, when he came to us as a guest). *"And in this place will I give peace, saith the Lord of Hosts.* Not just 'shall be peace,' but peace given to those there and also to those who go there. It seemed, if I may say so, as if the Place were a sort of filling-up station of peace."

I think that is what all feel about it. There are quiet nooks where children may be gathered for talks; and their elders can, if they wish, listen unobserved to the words of Life, and where our trained nursing-brothers and sisters may share their pot of honey, as a patient once put it, with another. Often Kohila and the other nurses used to cross the little bridge which leads from us on the East to our comrades on the West, and looking across to the glorious hills which seem to border the Place of Healing, though they are several miles away, they would talk over the good time that every day brought nearer, when they would be ready to serve the suffering there.

But the good time seemed long in coming. Never since this work began has it been free from attack of some sort. That attack has been spiritual, and so cannot be described as it could be if it were a matter of bombs dropping on buildings and shattering them. The story will never be told of all that has happened to prevent the Place of Healing from being built, and, when built, from being used. But if it could be told, we should, I think, let old and simple words explain its existence and continuance, as indeed they explain the existence and continuance of all that anywhere continues in the teeth of opposition: "Because of a truth there is about the place a power of God. For He that hath His dwelling in heaven Himself hath His eyes upon that place, and helpeth it."

Near us is a little Muslim town whose headman we remember

as true to his word. He had promised to come to see us one day, but could not get a cart. So he walked. He arrived tired but, "I promised, so I came," was all he said. It was his hour for prayer; we lent him a Persian mat and he went into the House of Prayer and knelt down there. The clear emptiness of the House charmed him. "No figures, no pictures," he said approvingly. We had thought of having the Good Shepherd picture, but had decided against it because of the Muslims and Hindus who for opposite reasons, might misunderstand. We were glad then that we had done so. There was nothing to explain. There were flowers, of course; but flowers need no explanation.

The old Muslim came sometimes on the Lord's Day, and worshipped with us. Once, pleased by something in the Service, he exclaimed aloud, "Excellent! Excellent!" to the astonishment of the children. He slept with a Bible under his pillow and we know that he read it; but there was no confession of Christ.

Soon after coming to us our doctor-guest, Murray Webb-Peploe, opened a dispensary in that town and the two men became friends. The old Muslim would look at his younger brother with almost paternal eyes, and as he patted his shoulder, chuckle comfortably, "A guest is he? Nay, *sonthum!*" It was he who found the fitting Indian name for him: "Call him *Friend of God*, for that is what he is," he said. Friend of God had served in the Great War under the General who wrote from the battlefield to his wife, "I ask daily for aid, not merely in making the plan, but in carrying it out, and this I hope I shall continue to do until the end of all things which concern me on earth. I think it is this Divine help which gives me tranquillity of mind and enables me to carry on without feeling the strain of responsibility to be too excessive. I try to do no more than do my best and trust to God." * The words might have been written by him to whom Kohila had already offered the fealty of her faithful heart.

---

* Earl Haig of Bemersyde

The doctor Sittie of the Place (Great Help is her Tamil name) † was also much beloved. And so were the nurses who had been given to us, and who at that time were studying Tamil in preparation for the new work. And happy vistas opened as we and our children talked of what was soon to be; and as the foundations were laid of each new building and the plans began to be more or less understood, there was exultation and wonder too.

For it is not a little thing to see one's future opening before one, slowly unrolling like a scroll illuminated with a thousand colours of joy and expectation. "Love has a marvellous property of feeling in another," and the suffering and lonely people whom Kohila had already seen, caused this "feeling in another" so to increase that she became more and more earnest to be fitted to serve. "I cannot remember her ever being slack," writes one who watched her life. "What she did she did with her whole heart. In all her work she was preparing for the Place of Spiritual Healing."

By this time she knew, and all the nurses-in-training knew, that it was not an easy thing to be a good nurse. I expect it is difficult everywhere, but in the Tropics where it is so hard to keep places clean, and where heat for months at a time doubles toil, it is distinctly difficult to be always what one ought to be. But perhaps only those who have experienced the difficulty know just what it is, or with what those who were training these young girls had to contend as a matter of course. Some will remember that during the War a certain official tried to persuade the Arabian leader Feisal (afterward King of Iraq) to undertake the impossible; he said that it would end the war at once if Feisal made his men climb about the precipitous country like goats and tear up the railway. "Feisal, angry at the metaphor (impolite in Arabic), looked at Bremond's six feet of comfortable body, and asked if he had ever tried to 'goat' himself."

†Christian Rogan.

I expect one has to "goat" oneself, before one can understand much about any such matter.

But far more difficult than the outward was the inward. And sometimes now that she was head-nurse her old temptations assailed Kohila again. A piercing sentence in a little book written privately for ourselves about this time, called *If*, alludes to it.

If the care of a soul (or a community) be entrusted to me, and I consent to subject it to weakening influences, because the voice of the world—my immediate Christian world—fills my ears, then I know nothing of Calvary Love.

Some in her own little world would say if she weakened, "How loving she is!" but what would her Lord say? That was the question which she had to face not once or twice, but often, for everything in her leaned towards love. But action that would lead to others' loss was not true love—she had learned that now.

The last of the "ifs" had a word for her too : *If I covet any place on earth but the dust at the foot of the Cross, then I know nothing of Calvary Love.*

And there were the common tests of common life: tests of patience with careless younger ones; tests of courage when hard things had to be done and there was pressure of work; tests of humility when her own imperfections rose up and confronted her. "The tests of the Spirit may try us; let us welcome them. They show us what God would have us to be. They show us what He will help us to be."

And there is a secret discipline appointed for every man and woman whose life is lived for others. No one escapes that discipline, nor would wish to escape it; nor can any shelter another from it. And just as we have seen the bud of a flower close round the treasure within, folding its secret up, petal by petal, so we have seen the soul that is chosen to serve, fold round its secret and hold it fast and cover it from the eyes of man. The petals of the soul are silence.

It was so with Kohila when she saw some of her school - fellows married and with dear children about them, and felt that for her that was not to be; for she knew and was sure that for her the other way was appointed; and He who had called her to that other way satisfied her heart. I think these words tell her thoughts :

> *If Thy dear Home be fuller, Lord,*
> *For that a little emptier*
> *My house on earth, what rich reward*
> *That guerdon were.*

26. THE STONE - BREAKER

(The old man, Sir Nameless, hears from the Shepherd of the great and noble stream that flows from the well he has guarded):

Wondering, the old man pondered these sayings. Slowly his eyes brightened as a fond thought came to his lips in words:

"Do they speak of me? Do they know who guards the well?"

Tenderly the Shepherd looked into the old man's eyes, tenderly he answered him:

"Nay, they know nothing of thee. What they know is the King's Bounty, what they see is the King's smile."

Then Constant looked, fearing to see a shadow fall upon the old man's eager hope. But the old man was looking into the Shepherd's face, and the shadow never came again. Instead his hope brightened into joy as he clasped his hands together and cried:

"And that is enough! O my heart, surely it is enough! It is ten thousand times more than enough!" And from that moment some thought which had troubled him long, troubled him no more.

Sir Knight of the Splendid Way, W.E.Cule.

"Thee must never say," said the wise and well-loved Robert Wilson of Keswick, as we drove in the gig along a Cumberland road many years ago, "thee must never even let thyself think, 'I have won that soul for Christ.'"

And he pulled up the old horse, Charlie, and stopped near a stone-breaker, who, squatting beside his pile of stones, was hammering steadily.

"I will tell thee a story," the dear old man said, pointing with his whip to the stone-breaker who tapped stolidly on and never looked up. "There was one who asked a stone-breaker at work by the roadside, 'Friend, which blow broke the stone?' And the stone-breaker answered, *'The first one, and the last one, and every one between.'"*

Perhaps among the influences that helped to shape, not Kohila only, but all of us, this story has its part, for I cannot remember ever hearing even the most ardent say anything contrary to the spirit of that story; nor have we ever made any list of the souls won by the Grace of the Lord—for whatsoever is done, He is the Doer of it.

Some of us have had the joy of "the first blow," if such a word may be used for an influence invisible and often so gentle; some have shared in the "every one between," and rejoiced to share. Some have had the chance to give the last blow that breaks the stone.

The joy of the winner and helper of souls is something apart from every other joy, but it is tarnished the moment the *I* comes in. God save us from our *I*.

Once among Kohila's patients was a young girl whom she had first loved as a little child in the nursery, when she was the Accal in charge.

Later on this child went through a difficult patch, as so many do, and finally, having passed through it, she became as Kohila had once been, a helping younger sister in a nursery.

One day as we talked together this young girl told of how Kohila had helped her, and of how she had learned to conquer the temptations that came to weaken her as she ran her race. "I sing this to myself," she said. "This" was a rhyme written to help our younger girls and boys to understand what self-discipline meant. Their Annãchie, Peace of God, had set it to a simple chant-like tune, for no Indian forgets anything that has sung itself into the mind; and she began to chant softly:

When I refuse the easy thing for love of my dear Lord,
And when I choose the harder thing for love of my dear Lord,
And do not make a fuss or speak a single grumbling word,
That is discipline.

When everything seems going wrong and yet I will not grouse,
When it is hot, and I am tired and yet I will not grouse,
But sing a song and do my work in school and in the house,
That is discipline.

When Satan whispers, "Scamp your work," to say to him,
   "I won't,"
When Satan whispers, "slack a bit," to say to him, "I won't,"
To rule myself and not to wait for others' Do and don't ,
That is discipline.

When I look up and triumph over every sinful thing,
The things that no one knows about, the cowardly, selfish thing,
And when with heart and will I live to please my glorious King,
That is discipline.

To trample on that curious thing inside me that says "I,"
To think of others always, never, never of that "I,"
To learn to live according to my Saviour's word, "Deny,"
That is Discipline.

Which blow broke the stone?

Her prayer-friend at home? Kohila, who, as Accal in her nursery and then as nurse in hospital, influenced her life? The Accals, such as one whose name means Perfection, and Rukma (Radiance), who helped her through her difficult patch? The Sitties, whose self-forgetful lives inspired her? The Annāchie, who taught the little chant that came to her rescue in moments of stress, and who led her and many another in these paths uphill? Those who in workroom and office did the thousand unseen things without which this family could not go on?

Which blow broke the stone?
The first one and the last one and every one between.

Among several of whom we know whom Kohila helped to win (and here it chanced that hers was the last blow) was a woman from an unresponsive village who had never been moved even to inquire about the Way. Our young nursery-nurses had often talked with her and tried to interest her, but in vain. They were "simply talking", she thought, and she turned an unconcerned and uncomprehending face upon them till she saw Kohila nursing a sick baby. She said nothing for a while. Then one day she said to her, "Why do you do it? Why do you work for this baby night and day? What makes you do it?"

"It is nothing in me," said Kohila; "it is the love of my Lord Jesus. It is He who gives me love for this baby."

"I have heard talk about Him," said the woman, "but I thought it was only talk; now I have seen, and I know it is not mere talk." And she listened to the Gospel, and the Lord opened her heart, and she came to Him in truth, though she knew what it would cost when she returned home.

Two months after she had returned home—a strong woman —she was dead. That is all we know, except that death for her meant the end of what she had known must come: sharp persecution for the sake of her new-found Lord; not peace, but a sword.

"There were others. There was Mercy of God, who came to us too ill to recover, and to whom Seetha Sittie was the first to speak of the love of our Lord Jesus," said a young nurse, as we talked of Kohila and of her earnest use of every opportunity. "Kohila was one who often used to sing to her and talk with her.. She asked for baptism and she was baptized; and she lived after that in great peace till our Lord Jesus came for her and then she said, 'Jesus! Lord Jesus!' and went Home to Him."

Which blow broke the stone?

The first one and the last one and every one between. Those who prayed and gave, and so made it possible for us to save children and build nurseries and hospital; the builders; the doctors and nurses; and, looking farther back, all who influenced the young girls whose lives and witness showed forth their love of the Lord.

And to them all the word is, "Let them exult before God: let them be delighted with joy," for "the King of the forces of the beloved, of the Beloved, will even grant them for the beauty of the house, to divide the spoils." *

We have seen many victories of Divine Love. Perhaps Mimosa is best known to our friends. And when she entered into the Presence of her Lord, and in the Place of Healing and the House of Prayer the girls played the chimes—the Joy-bells, we call them—we could all but see her pleasure and surprise, as one and another of her unknown fellow-lovers welcomed her into the beauty of the House.

---

*Ps.68.3, 12. LXX.

The first one and the last one and every one between. Those who prayed and gave, and so made it possible for us to save children and build nurseries and hospitals the builders the doctors and nurses, and looking farther back, all who influenced the young girls whose lives and witness showed forth their love of the Lord.

And to them all the word is, "Let them exult before God; let them be delighted with joy," for "the King of the forces of the beloved, of the Beloved, will even grant them for the beauty of the house, to divide the spoils."

We have seen many victories of Divine Love. Perhaps Mimosa is best known to our friends. And when she entered into the Presence of her Lord, and in the Place of Healing and the House of Prayer, the girls played the chimes — the Joy-bells, we call them — we could all but see her pleasure and surprise, as one and another of her unknown fellow-lovers welcomed her into the beauty of the House.

As for my child, our children come, come, but in deed and in truth to Him who said, "Suffer the little children..."

Hine to one and to all over, but yet together... She come... She is our Lord, our Father, our Lord... Watchful God — Our kind Father to protect us, to teach us...

27. THROUGH DIMNESS
TO CLEARNESS

He mistrusted his powers, till he remembered that he was only a servant of great allies. A servant—the humblest of servants. He was not architect or builder, nor even a labourer with a hod, but something lowlier still, and in his lowliness was strength.

A Prince of the Captivity, John Buchan.

Soul, be steadfast to the last,
Till the fight of fights is o'er.
When thine ALL away is cast
Loss is gain for evermore.

Brand, Henrik Ibsen.

ONE Spring morning in Japan, as I stood looking at an almond tree in bud, a Japanese said to me, "We call it the Waking-tree, for it wakens and watches the other trees open in blossom." "What seest thou?" his Lord asked Jeremiah, and he answered, "I see the rod of an almond tree" (a shaked tree, a Wakeful-tree). So his Lord answered him, "Thou hast well seen; for I watch over My word to perform it" (shoked, watchful).

As, child by child, our children come to us, they are dedicated to Him who redeemed them. All that the upper and nether springs meant to us in the early days is still our heart's desire; we claim the fulfilment of the promise implied in the question of our heavenly Caleb, "What wouldest thou?" And we trust Him to be watchful over His word to perform it. Shivvati, I cried. Shammata, Thou heardest. Shaked, the Wakeful-tree. Shoked, the Watchful God—Our kind Father sometimes teaches us as we teach our little ones by catch-words and pictures, perhaps lest we forget to be simple.

Among the girls and younger women, Indian and foreign, there is a Company known as the Sisters of the Common Life.* No one is ever asked to join it. But quietly, with no fuss or flourish of trumpets, the more earnest find their way to this Company, which means in a new sense the dedication of the life. For it is to the Sisters we look for the costliest co-operation. The most difficult things that come to be done belong by right to them.

There are now several Companies led by different members of the Fellowship. Life, that great tester, is patiently proving them. Meanwhile we hold fast to the word about the almond tree, and we cast not away our confidence which hath great recompense of reward.

There is always a special attack on those at the centre of any work, whose first object is to satisfy the heart of our Lord, and who have said to Him, "I will be occupied in Thy commandments." And some who, after joining, and thus openly pledging themselves to an unlimited obedience, find that for a time it is as if a mist descended upon them and their sky clouded over and they hardly know where they are. At first they think there is something wrong with the circumstances in which they are set, and are ready to ask for some other work: "Anything but this." But if they are sincere, they soon learn to pray from the depths of their hearts, "Let me not be ashamed, O Lord"; and to count as golden grains each word of a Scripture like this, "My heart rejoiceth because Thou art so willing to help," Luther's translation of Ps. 13. 5. Also the Septuagint of Isaiah 57.15, *The Most High resting in the Holies and giving patience to the faint-hearted and giving life to the broken-hearted.* For, remembering who used that ancient version, we often use it, and find that a different rendering of a familiar word discovers some new beauty. It is as if one turned a jewel in one's hand. But the Bible is full of such jewels.

Kohila passed through this test of faith. Dependence on feelings

---

* *Gold Cord*, ch. 22.

had to be left behind her before she could go on to the place where
everything was at her Lord's feet, and in all things He had the pre-
eminence.

Long before she was born, the leader of the Manchester City
Mission brought out a book in which he set certain songs. One of
these, meant to be sung as a solo, dealt with this dullness of spirit which
can so distress the true follower of the Radiant Christ:

Sometimes I catch sweet glimpses of His face, but that is all.
Sometimes He looks on me and seems to smile, but that is all.
Sometimes He speaks a passing word of peace, but that is all.
Sometimes I think I hear His loving voice upon me call.

And is this all He meant when first He said "Come unto Me"?
Is there no deeper, more enduring, rest in Him for thee?
Is there no steadier light for thee in Him? O come and see.
Is there no deeper, more enduring, rest in Him for thee?

Nay, do not wrong Him by thy heavy thoughts, but love His love.
Do thou full justice to His tenderness, His mercy prove.
Take Him for what He is, O take Him all, and look above;
And do not wrong Him by thy heavy thought, but love His love.

Christ and His love shall be thy blessed all for evermore.
Christ and His light shall shine on all thy ways for evermore.
Christ and His peace shall keep thy troubled soul for evermore.
Christ and His love shall be thy blessed all for evermore.

Not in one sudden outpouring, but rather with the quietness
of light that falls upon our Western hills and waters at eventide, a loveliness
that she had often watched, Kohila came to the place where Christ and
His love became her blessed All. She was still a shy soul. Deliverance
from the kind of reserve which holds one back as by a silken thread
was not hers yet, but it was coming. And those who loved her saw her
opening, not as our blue morning-glories and our white moon-flowers

open, as though moved by one gentle, all-pervading impulse, but more as our large purple passion-flowers open, a little at a time. Their sepals and petals move separately and slowly, and there is a kind of stickiness about their stamens; they do not at once shake themselves free. But in the end, as you watch you see them, and every other part of that symbolic flower, each in its several place. And the whole flower opens its heart to you and pours out its perfume.

It is then that the words of the song are at last fulfilled: Christ and His love become the blessed All of that happy soul for evermore.

This steadfast going through dimness to clearness was vital to the spiritual life of many a young girl then, as it has been since, in the life of many a boy. It was a discipline of the spirit that cannot be omitted in any true story. Some of those who went through it alone, surrounded by scoffing Hindus, returned after that searching experience so established in faith that their lives have shone steadfastly ever since. One of God's Apelles *("Apelles that tested man in Christ. The Lord knows, not we, the tests he stood")* has said of the missionary, "He must be sure of his calling. In the dark days when the gate of life's garden opens on to the olives of Gethsemane and no stars shine in the sky, his great resource will be, 'the Father who hath sent me hath not left me alone.'" And the words are as true where a young girl, who would never dream of calling herself a missionary, is concerned. For she is as much her Lord's Sent-one as any other, and as much as any other needs to be able to say, *And He who sent me is with me,* when the sky darkens and the waves roll up, and the old words take on a new meaning : " No Crown but by the Cross. No life eternal but through death."

So Kohila did not ask for other work. Nothing was changed, and yet everything was different. And she learned another of the lessons set to all who pass through the schoolrooms of God: Do not ask for a change in your circumstances. Ask only that nothing shall come between you and His light. The same mountains, water, grasses may compose the landscape of your life, but you have gone a little farther along the road; you see those mountains, water and grasses a little differently, and the whole atmosphere of the place is new; it is heavenly. Where is the gloom that hung upon your ways not half an hour ago? Those same ways "shine like light; they go on and shine," is another lovely word from the Septuagint.

" O but praising God is light!"

28. A NOTE

When the spirit of discipline has once been infused, it is no less important to pay careful attention to its maintenance.

It engenders a spirit of calmness in emergency. The same spirit which keeps a disciplined man at his post when all his comrades have fallen, will keep a man brave and cool in the midst of emergency, panic and disaster. In other words, discipline renders a man more capable of facing the changes and chances of human existence.

It produces a certain determination and firmness of character. A disciplined man, who has been given a difficult task to accomplish, is more likely to carry it through to a successful conclusion than the undisciplined man who may be turned aside at the first obstacle. The man of discipline has learnt to resist, bear up, hold on, in spite of all difficulties.

In a word, the object and the result of true discipline is to inspire men with bravery, firmness, patience, and with sentiment of honour.

The Life of John Rushworth Earl Jellicoe, Admiral Sir Reginald Bacon.

THE influences brought to bear upon this group of workers were meant to weld into one band, disciplined women from whom the hardest could be asked without hesitation, and without careful preparation. Someone has said that courage in strife is common, but the courage which can face the ultimate defeat of a life of good-will— that is different, that is victory. We are not working for love or gratitude (though often we meet the loving and the grateful). We wanted to be able to count on some who would not crumple up under disappointment, but whose self-discipline was such that they would stand fast and carry on however things were.

And, to quote Cheltenham again, we wanted to teach them to be women of whom it could be said, "Nothing for self, all for those committed to their care, their whole life arranged so as best to further their work." Here also, we felt the need of a constant renewal of vitality, if we were to be a living thing, not a machine. The weekly meetings for the Sisters of the Common Life were intended to help towards that end.

There are some years that stand out in memory as difficult beyond others. The year that this company was formed was such a year, but "It is the temper of the highest hearts to strive most upwards when they are most burdened," and we wanted that temper, no other; so we sometimes studied together what we always thought of as our Pattern. A brief note of the first of these studies by some chance found its way to one who afterwards offered to the Fellowship. She felt in tune with it and kept it, and has now given it to help Kohila's story.

This is the Note:

And look that thou make them after the pattern which was shewed thee in the Mount.

What was the Pattern that was showed us in the Mount? A work whose heart is set on the glory of the Lord. A work whose workers are all wholly the Lord's. A work full of love and joy and hope and peace: "And all things were done in such excellent methods, and I cannot tell how, but things in the management of them seemed to cast a smile." A work hidden from the eye of man, but open to the eye of God, at all points searched by Him, lest at any time lesser aims creep in and the whole became defiled. A work whose needs are supplied by the Lord Himself, in answer to prayer based upon His word, upon which He has caused us to hope.

This was the Pattern which was showed us in the Mount; Lord, grant us grace to remember it and follow it.

Perils in connection with this work—discouragement, when we seem to aspire in vain; hopelessness, when grieved to the heart over lapses in those who did run well; unwatchfulness, if for a moment we slip into the snare of the praise of man; a sore spirit if we listen too much to the blame of man; a slack spirit if we rest on our oars even for only a day; the spirit of fear when supplies run low and we are buffeted by many temptations. From all these perils, good Lord, deliver us.

Cause us to abound in hope, and to watch as those who must give account.

Hide us from the scourge of the tongue, but teach us how to find any help there is to be found in criticism and innuendo.

Make us far more intensely in earnest, and cause us to press on—on to the goal, even unto the end.

29. STAND UP TO THE DIFFICULTIES OF LIFE

Let us, then, have the full courage of renunciation; let us rise above the surface of the surrounding mediocrity. The least regret, the shortest glance backwards would be more than weakness; it would be cowardice and treason ... Stand up to the difficulties of life .... Maintain peace; keep your life high above passing events.

Père Didon.

THIS chapter and the following three are for those who care to know what lies behind the words, spiritual training; I suggest that they be omitted by any to whom this is not a matter of special interest.

In India you may easily gather a cheery crowd for a motor-bus drive to a distant village (in old days it was a much hotter and more toilsome matter to reach it), you may even find some eager to trudge on foot if "a preaching" be at the end of the walk. And you may feel, "Now at last I am doing a real missionary's work. Nothing else counts."

But if behind you there are not some who laboured that you may enter into their labours, there may be things of which you know nothing going on underground, and making that successful preaching less pleasing to your Lord's pure eyes than to yours. And the same is true of all forms of service and witness.

When first this work began we had a band of evangelists but no Sisters of the Common Life or any remotely like them; and we were constantly baffled by the habit of even true Christians to see in success—only in success—the blessing of God. If what the world calls failure or any kind of reverse occurred, the Lord was not with us—that was the general attitude. "If that child recovers I shall know that the favour of God is upon this work of saving young children from the temples. If not, then—" The sentence was not always finished,

143

but we knew its ending. If the Good Shepherd gathers a lamb in His arms and carries it out of sight, then we should give up trying to save any single one of the countless lambs, who were as helpless as the lamb of which David told when he said, There came a lion and a bear and took a lamb out of the flock. The lamb must be left to its fate.

So we set ourselves to build up a company on a foundation which could not be shaken by any untoward event.

"In religion it matters nothing who says a thing or how beautifully he says it. The only question we ought to ask is this—Is it written in the Bible? what saith the Lord?" We had found our "Thus saith the Lord," and were at rest about the rightness of going on; and we had found countless proofs of His Presence in the difficulties that often follow obedience. All this was familiar ground. Something less obvious (for it was hidden like a nut in its shell) lay in the story of the three kings in their war against Moab.

When the King of Moab rebelled against the King of Israel, and the Kings of Judah and Edom came to Jehoram's help, they had to decide by which way they should go up against the enemy.

There were two possible ways: The first ran north of the Dead Sea, crossed the Jordan and the boundary river Arnon, and so entered Moab from the north. The second went round the southern coast of the Dead Sea, passed through the northern ranges of the mountains of Edom, and entered Moab from the south. This was the longer and more arduous way, but was chosen perhaps "because the Moabites from their confidence in the inaccessibility of their southern boundary would hardly expect an attack from that side." A river flowed through the valley the army must traverse, so there was no reason to fear lack of water: that stream seldom failed. But it failed now. There was no water for the host and for the cattle that followed them. And the King of Israel said, "Alas! that the Lord hath called these kings together, to deliver them into the hand of Moab!" But Jehoshaphat said, "Is there not here a prophet of the Lord that we may enquire of the Lord by him?" And the prophet said, "Bring me a minstrel. And it came to pass, when the minstrel played, that the hand of the Lord came upon him, and he said, Thus saith the Lord, Make this valley full of ditches. For thus saith the Lord, Ye shall not see wind, neither shall ye see rain; yet that valley shall be filled with water, that ye may drink, both ye, and your cattle, and your beasts. And this is but a light thing in the sight of the Lord: He will deliver the Moabites also into your hand."

So, as we of India say, the sap of the matter was this: if our Father's timely succour was given to men whose trouble, so far as we know, did not come directly because of the obedience to a command (no command is recorded), how much more surely will it be given to carry us over difficulties which arise because our hearts are set "to all meeting of His wishes"? Do not look back upon guidance because of unexpected difficulties. To do that is to weaken the line along its whole length. "Do nothing without advice, and when thou hast once done, repent not." Or better, do nothing without giving time to seek and to receive Divine direction. (Cause me to know the way wherein I should walk; for I lift up my soul unto Thee. Teach me to do Thy will.) And when thou hast once done, repent not.

But it may be that the Spirit is blocking the way. If so, He will not leave you in doubt. Or it may be that the Power of Darkness is allowed to have authority over that hour. ("This is your hour and the power of darkness.") If that be so, wait in faith. The hour will pass and the glory of the Lord will be made manifest. Then the way will clear and you will be free to go on. Let nothing forbid you. You cannot meet anything that was unforeseen by your Leader; and though a thousand streams dry up, He has water to fill a thousand more.

Just one last lovely touch: "A great rainfall on the western mountains of Edom far from the camp of those thirsty men and beasts would fill the watercourse" —so Keil. *In the morning there came water by the way of Edom and the country was filled with water.*

30. THEIR KING KNEW

He will remember that obloquy is a necessary ingredient in the composition of all true glory; he will remember that it was not only in the Roman *custome,* but it is in the nature and constitution of things, that calumny and abuse are essential parts of triumph.

The Life of John Rushworth Earl Jellicoe, Admiral Sir Reginald Bacon.

SOME are wonderfully created. They can go through a thick flight of stinging arrows and hardly feel them. It is as if they were clad in fine chain-armour.

Others are made differently. The arrows pierce, and most sharply if they be shot by friends. The very tone of a voice can depress such a one for a week. (It can uplift, too; for the heart that is open to hurt is also very open to love.)

The Indian has by nature no chain-armour, and some of us can understand just what that means. But if we are to be God's knights, we must learn to go through flights of arrows, and so the teaching which was set on fashioning warriors, not weaklings, often dealt with this.

There was a day—it was before the girls who were now being forged into a team had begun to be—when Walker of Tinnevelly sat alone in his study reading the copy of a document addressed to the Archbishop of Canterbury. It was a petition against him and one or two other true men who had stood by him in his efforts to cut certain cankers out of this South Indian Church. It was an amazing composition, cruel and false because so ignorant.

He came out from his study that day looking very white, and his eyes were like dark fires. But he went straight on like a man walking through cobwebs stretched across his path. And what does it matter now? He has seen his Lord's face. *All that troubles is only for a moment. Nothing is important but that which is eternal.*

Soon after this, one of my brothers sent me Ibsen's *Brand*, with some lines from Plato therein.

A book is a friend to be shared with a friend, and I shared *Brand* with the man who had been so strangely maligned. When he returned the book I found these and other similar lines heavily under-scored: "Hear, ye people, compromise is the very Prince of Lies. . . . Aye, the times for greatness call just because they are so small. . . . If I'm to keep my soul's religion whole, it won't go into your State pigeon-hole. . . . With us a sabre is something innocently blunt. . . . An altar's something to put cash on : that's our extremest Cross and Passion."

Slipped into the book opposite Plato's lines I found these verses; "Plato Christianised," the writer called them:

> *My glorious Leader, dost Thou deign*
> *To place me in the fight?*
> *Then is my duty grandly plain,*
> *To quit me as Thy knight.*
>
> *Never will I desert the post*
> *Thy favour has assigned;*
> *Or pale before the embattled host*
> *Surging before, behind.*
>
> *Let me Thy battle never shame*
> *By craven compromise,*
> *But play the man for Thy great Name,*
> *And win the victor's prize.*

A few years later two friends who were staying with us, and who, of course, knew nothing of that petition, which naturally carried no weight, suggested that some homeletters telling of things as they were should be gathered into a book. A London publisher chanced to visit Dohnavur, saw the MS. and asked for it. Without a thought of the commotion that would follow, that MS. was put into his hands.

At home "a book like this will gravely injure the cause of missions," was the general word—and nothing had been further from the thought of the writer than that. In India there was a great furore, and a meeting was held to consider some way of getting the offender out of the country as soon as possible. But somehow the meeting could not agree about the best way to effect that, or perhaps the Lord blew upon it, for nothing happened. Some time afterwards the one who had been the most vigorous member of that meeting came to Dohnavur; and as he sat on the verandah of the nursery - courtyard, loving, trustful little children gathered round him, climbed on his lap and called him, "Dear older brother." And the kind heart in him melted. He told the whole story. "Can you ever forgive me?" he said.

But what was there to forgive? It was only a mistake. And what did it matter now? *All that troubles is only for a moment. Nothing is important but that which is eternal.*

There was another little incident that had taught the one who was teaching these girls something of the unimportance of the dust of words: One of the first meetings she was asked to take in India was for English soldiers belonging to a South Indian cantonment. It was supposed to be a Temperance meeting, but Temperance was hardly mentioned. The soldiers needed something that went much deeper. That meeting was reported in the Parish magazine. An address had been given on the benefits of alcohol. It had come as a pleasant surprise, the writer said, to hear from a missionary that alcohol was beneficial.

For a minute a quite young missionary felt this rather staggering. And then suddenly the thought came, "It won't matter fifty years hence, so what does it matter now?" *Nothing is important but that which is eternal.*

These stories and others, straight from life, and so close to them too, helped that little company to come to the place where they understood, and made their own, this truth: sometimes circumstances are so that we must be misunderstood, we cannot defend ourselves. We lie open to blame, and yet we may know ourselves clear towards God and man in that particular matter. Then consider Him who endured. They laid to His charge things that He knew not. Remember how often we are thought of as better than we are. The blame "missed only the right blot, 'Tis very just they blame the thing that's not."

The Marcus Aurelius attitude may have to be ours for a while. Somebody wounds you in the gymnasium, he said; you are not offended, but you "quietly get out of his way. Something like this let thy behaviour be in all other parts of life."

Or, put in ancient Tamil form, "If you speak with such a one, in replying he will pervert your words. To slip away from him as best you can, is well." "Beware of him," said St. Paul.

But if you love the one who wounded you in the gymnasium, it is a heart-breaking thing to have to do this, and you cannot rest there, you cannot rest, and yet you must not fret; you must wait in the patience of hope till confidence can be again, that which used to be, that which is, when

> High and low and lower,
> Put into parts, doth keep in one consent,
> Congreeing in a full and natural close,
> Like music.

"In refusing to be put out or annoyed, you are taking God's hand in yours, and once you feel God's hand, or the hand of any one who loves good, in yours, let pity take the place of irritation, let silence take the place of a hasty answer. Charity suffereth long and is kind, especially to the unkind" —so Edward Wilson.

This is something that it is difficult for the sensitive Indian to understand. It is, indeed, impossible unless "the habit and spirit of discipline" be deeply engrained. At the time we were meeting in the quietness of this secluded place a life was being lived in the blaze of publicity on these same lines. It is written of Earl Jellicoe, that throughout the dark days which followed the Battle of Jutland, he kept silence; his self-discipline prevented him from retorting. He had spoken of discipline as something less obvious and tangible than is commonly supposed, but more real and deeply engrained, and not only the practice of discipline, but, still more, the habit and spirit of discipline, was what men saw in him. There are few nobler words than *"Noblesse oblige,"* few more compelling than, "Hold thee still in the Lord, and abide patiently upon Him." Never retort. "Thou shalt answer for me, O Lord, my God."

But often the more generous way is to take generosity for granted in those who are making life painful, and, like Peter when he met his misjudging friends, rehearse the matter from the beginning and expound it by order unto them. If this fails, then return to silence.

Sometimes we read words from the ancient Tamil classics (rays from the light that lighteth every man that cometh into the world), Afflictive indeed is friendship with the uncongenial—that is admitted, but although you bite the sugar-cane, crush it till its joints are broken, grind it and express its juice, it will still be sweet. The noble never retaliate.*

---

* Compare Hecuba (*The Tragedies of Euripides*) translated by Dr.Way.
Always among men.
The caitiff nothing else than evil is,

A beautiful quatrain is about silence where a disappointing friend is concerned : when those to whom we clung disappoint, keep the sad secret hid, cling to them still. The growing grain has husks; the water has its foam; flowers have a scentless outer sheath of leaves.

It is wonderful to have so rich a language from which to draw; Dr. Pope considers the writer of the Tamil *Kurral* to be one of the great geniuses of the world, though he be known only in Southern India. There are lines in that book which strike deep: To feel doubt of a friend once trusted is a wound that nought can heal, but

> What his own soul has felt as bitter pain,
> From making others feel should man abstain.

And a lovely old proverb says, "Though it be the nux vomica, wish that it may be green." Thank God a friend, even a disappointing friend, is not nux vomica.

So we always came to this: Go on loving : "By the words of Thy lips have I guarded me from hard ways" (the Septuagint rendering of Ps.77.4). Go on praying: Pray for them that despitefully use you. (Our Lord does not say, Wait till they are sorry for treating you so.)   Go on forgiving: "Longsuffering is the spirit which will not be tired out of pardoning, hoping, loving; bearing with one another and forgiving one another, if any one has a grievance against any one; for you are erring sinners still, and *may* give each other occasion for such victories of good

---

> The noble, noble; nor 'neath fortune's stress
> Marreth his nature, but is good alway.
> By blood, or nurture, is the difference made?
> Sooth, gentle nurture bringeth lessoning
> In nobleness; and whoso learns this well
> By honour's touchstone knoweth baseness too.

over evil." Above all, consider Him from whom the worst that man could do could only wring the prayer, "Father, forgive them; for they know not what they do."

Be careful also of your after-thinking as well as of your after-talking about any who have misjudged you. "The hill-man thinks upon the beauty of his hills; the farmer thinks upon his fields that have yielded him rich crops; the good think on the boons bestowed by worthy men; the base man's thoughts are fixed on the abuse he has received," is another old Tamil saying. Do not feed unloving thoughts. Remember His word, "I forgave thee all that debt."

For the eternal substance of a thing never lies in the thing itself, but in the quality of our reaction towards it. If in hard times we are kept from resentment, held in silence and filled with inward sweetness, that is what matters. The event that distressed us will pass from memory as a wind that passes and is gone. But what we were while the wind was blowing upon us has eternal consequences.

And watch for the comforts of God. When Earl Jellicoe was being misunderstood by the nation he served so faithfully, a letter came from King George, whose keen sea-sense had penetrated the mist which had bemused the general public. His letter heartened the Fleet. What did anything matter now? "Their King knew."

Here again we were on familiar ground. Once during a time of entangling distress just such a letter came to us, heartening, because it was so strong and so understanding: "There is such a thing as a 'brasen wall' as well as a 'pillar of iron,' and which belongs to our heavenly calling. The temple of the Lord, and such works as we are seeking to carry on, must be surrounded by the unity of a brasen wall, and the workers themselves must realise that they are each one of them a living part of that 'wall.' Only thus can the work itself be a 'pillar' of truth for God in the world." And the writer told us that he was "claiming for us the unbinding of the spirit from that painful pre-occupation" which is one of the devil's favourite snares at such a time, because it so effectively keeps the servant from what should be his single occupation. "Difficulties are many and great," our friend wrote later, "and the more we go on, the more the 'bruised heel' seems to become a reality. But such is the communion to which we are called, and thus only the power of His resurrection rests on us."

The prayer of that friend (Founder of the Ecole Biblique, Geneva, where men and women are trained to be warriors on whom their comrades can count for the things that matter most) was very wonderfully answered. "I am shut up, and I cannot come forth," had all but been the word of our hearts, so binding can grief be. Now it was as in a prison long ago, when a light shined, and chains fell off. We were set at liberty from what had been indeed a painful preoccupation and our word was then, O Lord, truly I am Thy servant: Thou hast loosed my bonds. I will offer to Thee the sacrifice of thanksgiving. Return unto thy rest, O my soul; for the Lord hath dealt bountifully with thee.

Why should we ever be bound? Of what account is anything if our King knows?

31. MUST. MUST NOT

The great fact which is often lost sight of, is that in a well-disciplined force the officers as well as the men are disciplined; that is to say, *each officer and man has conquered himself* and is therefore in a fit condition to subordinate his own wishes and desires in carrying out the orders given to him, which, as he knows, are meant to forward the cause for which they stand.

Life of John Rushworth Earl Jellicoe, Admiral Sir Reginald Bacon.

THERE was a time when everything turned upon whether we would or would not subordinate our own wishes and desires and carry through and put in execution all that was purposed and called for, in spite of opposition. (This is what Darby understands Ephesians 6. 13 to mean.) And in a cave in the Forest one who had gone there for a day's Quietness wrote down the searching thoughts that came. These "Must" and "Must Nots" were thereafter to influence our commonest duties and put iron into all our resolutions.

We must keep our windows open toward Jerusalem; not toward any place of earth, but toward Jerusalem—which means Gethsemane, and Calvary, and the Mount of Olives. The word is always, Walk before Me, and be thou perfect.

We must be very sensitive about any deviation from the Pattern shown in the Mount, not only for the carrying on of the work, but also for the conduct of our own lives. We must live more in the invisible, more consistently recognising its force for good and evil.

We must not be surprised by attack, as if it were a strange thing. We must be more spiritual in outlook and in expectation, more brave every way, more radiant.

We must not be distracted and deceived by the things that are

155

seen. "While we look not at the things which are seen" sometimes means, look through them as if they were transparent, and fix your eyes on the things that are not seen. It is these, the eternal things, that should govern our attitude towards everything with which we have to deal.

We must not dilute convictions or shrink back from obedience. Are your minds set upon righteousness, O ye congregation? The work of righteousness shall be peace; and the effect of righteousness quietness and assurance for ever.

We must not be moved by the small thoughts of to-day. Our Lord is made after the power of an endless life, and He brings that power to bear upon all that concerns us.

We must not sin against Love. Even though we may have to say what we believe to be true, we must refuse all belittling criticism of souls who have slipped, or people who have failed us, or the leadings of the past, or the field in which we are set, or the character of the people whom we have been sent to help.

We must hold fast together, drawing all in, if possible; if this be impossible, we must close up the line.

We must be more fearless in the speech that is steeped in love when we see in any one a yielding to a note which is not the note of the Spirit for this Fellowship. We must be frank with one another about this thing.

We must seek to live more with God than with man or woman.

We must go on to the deep places of prayer. My soul, wait thou only upon God. It is easy to slip into depending too much on companionship in prayer. The eager kindle the dull. I am dull. I lean towards the lighted spirit alongside and light my candle there. But we must not light the candle of prayer from the candle of another. O Flame of the Living God, kindle us direct. It must be so if the fire of prayer is to be true altar-fire.

Here there was a long parenthesis. (This does not make nothing of the help of human companionship. "Then Daniel went to his house and made the thing known to his companions that they would desire mercies of the God of heaven." Jonathan went to David, heart-sore after the Keilah experience, and strengthened his hands in God. Even our Lord seemed to miss companionship in prayer when it was not given : "Could ye not watch with Me one hour?" There is power in united prayer. The longing for it is not a mere human feeling. But the heart must not lean on it: my soul, wait thou only upon the Lord. Our Lord went on steadfastly without this help that night in Gethsemane. Paul in his Roman prison went on without it when he prayed, not the brief, easy prayer of the unburdened, but the long, lonely labour of conflict. And many a martyr and many held in bonds by illness, perhaps at home, perhaps in a great hospital, have had to learn to pray without the inspiration of numbers.)

Then we returned to our "we must": We must learn, as the Tamil proverb says, to plough deep rather than wide. Only God can plough both deep and wide.*

We must learn to live in our will, not in our feelings. This is essential for soldiership.

Such a way of working makes very stern demands. It does not show much for all that is put into it. (The foundations of a building never show at all; the seed slowly dying undergound does not show.) So the natural man becomes discouraged, and asks, "Is it worth while?"

---

* "There is but a certain quantity of spiritual force in any man. Spread it over a broad surface, the stream is shallow and languid; narrow the channel and it becomes a driving force."

Samuel Rutherford : *A Study*, Robert Gilmour.

God give it to us to detect the whisper of the serpent in such doubts and utterly to refuse them.

Where the things of the Father are concerned the word is, "Give thyself wholly to them"; "Be wholly in them"; "Be absorbed in them." If we are to do anything vital for the Kingdom, we must pay the price: we must be absorbed.

We must go further in the knowledge of His will about what is meant by, *And when thou hast shut thy door.* We must be eager for any loss for the sake of the gain that is not a luxury of the imagination, but something that we cannot do without if we are to keep very close behind our Lord.*

And there was the eternal "Must" of suffering, which always in the end is to the glory of God. Has any one in any land driven a deep furrow through the field that was his world, without suffering? Not one. Take two men, one in the seventeenth and one in the eighteenth centuries, whose lives mightily helped to stem the tide of godlessness—George Fox, Charles Wesley.

George Fox, as "stiff as a tree, and as pure as a bell, for we could never bow him," falsely accused, was thrust into a horrible dungeon among felons and moss-troopers. His surroundings were loathsome. "A filthy, nasty place it was, where men and women were put together in a very uncivil manner. Yet, bad as the place was, the prisoners were all made very loving and subject to me, and some of them were convinced of the Truth." And in the end, "I was never in prison that it was not the means of bringing multitudes out of their prisons," words that should be written in golden letters over every life that is caused to suffer, either in the flesh or the spirit, for righteousness sake.

---

* "My soul has kept very close behind Thee." Ps.63.8, LXX.S

And Charles Wesley, caught by a mob, hustled, struck, the life almost crushed out of him, but "I broke aloud into prayer." The end of that experience was, "I never saw such a chain of providences before; so many convincing proofs, that the hand of God is on every person and thing, overruling all as it seemeth Him good."

We must not expect to win souls or lead them on in Christian life without long travail. If it became Him for whom are all things and by whom are all things, in bringing many sons unto glory, to make the Captain of their salvation perfect through sufferings, who are we that we should expect easily to bring many sons (or daughters) to glory? "My little children, of whom I travail in birth again until Christ be formed in you," that is what we must expect. And when this travail comes we must go through with it, not try to escape from it. "And what shall I say? Father, save me from this hour; but for this cause came I unto this hour. Father, glorify Thy Name."

The last "we must" led to the Garden of Rest. "Now in the place where He was crucified there was a garden"; there is always a garden somewhere near the place of our sorest travail. We must find the way to that Garden.

> *There were two gardens in the land,*
> *And both lay on a hill,*
> *And one was called Gethsemane,*
> *The other was near Calvary;*
> *And both are with us still.*
>
> *Lord, when we climb our Olivet,*
> *Show us the garden there.*
> *And teach us how to kneel with Thee*
> *Beneath some ancient olive tree,*
> *And learn to pray Thy prayer.*

And when we climb the farther hill,
Where once the mighty Powers
Of hell defied Thee, lift our eyes
To where the peaceful garden lies,
That welcomed Thee with flowers.

32. OF ONE MIND IN AN HOUSE

The secret of his influence lay in a self-discipline that was as habitual as most men's habits are, an inner culture of mind and heart and will that gave his life a poise, so that he could not be untrue either to himself or his fellow-men.

Edward Wilson of the Antartic, Seaver.

The spirit of loyalty which unites every part of the Army must give it an additional strength in your hands; I heard from all sides what a happy army it is.

King George V to Earl Haig of Bemersyde.

WE have friends all over the world, and with many of them we are in close touch. But our power to do that which they count upon us to do depends on our inward unity, for a house divided against a house falleth. And so the words from the 1539 version of Psalm 68.6 were often in our hearts, "He is the God that maketh men to be of one mind in an house."

Such words brought us once more straight to the "Must" that stood like a block of granite in our path, that Must which is never softened by mosses growing over it, but stands out in all its naked firmness.

To be of one mind in an house is the happiest possible way to live ("I heard from all sides what a happy army it is"), and yet, if it be our chosen way, we must be keenly on the alert lest the enemy find a loophole and slip in, to our discomfiture. Quite a small loophole is enough for him.

Are we of one mind about following the Crucified?

If so, then as He was poor, so we would be poor. As He was made like unto his brethren, so we would be made like unto ours. As He was servant of all, so we would serve all. As He did not spare Himself, so we would not spare ourselves. As He wholly gave Himself,

161

so we would wholly give ourselves. As He loved unto the end, so we would love unto the end.

Are we of one mind about loyalty towards one another?

If so, we must pray for and work for that inner self-discipline which penetrates to the very core of being, and fortifies the soul against disloyalty. The thing the devil most fears is prayer, so he is perpetually trying to undermine the foundations of prayer; and one of these is loyalty. If only he succeeds there, then, though we may hold a dozen prayer-meetings a day, we have ceased to be a menace to his kingdom, and he is free to turn his attention elsewhere.

Are we of one mind about continuing to be a family, not an institution ?

If so, we must keep the family love quick and warm in our midst. We can do this only if we live close to the heart of God, and meet one another in Him, and delight to recognise Him in one another. The danger of becoming shallower in affection increases as we grow in numbers; it is worth while to give thought to the little things which nourish love, and that are to it what leaf and bud and blossom are to the growing tree, what colour is to form, and fragrance to the rose.

Are we of one mind about being on guard concerning the deadly foes of aggressive warfare, keenness and spiritual joy?

If so, one of the chief qualities we must ask from one another will be soldiership. We must seek to hold one another to the soldierly always and everywhere. This is something easier to write about than to do.

It touches the tendency to want something more comfortable than need be. We ought to be evidently people who belong to another Country, people who are quite clearly not anxious to make a soft nest for themselves or their loved ones, but to spend as little as possible upon themselves, so that they may have more to give to others. If this way of life be questioned, surely the answer is, Had there been a better way than the way of 2 Corinthians8. 9, would not our Lord have chosen that other way?

It touches what we sometimes think of as trifles such as table-talk. There would never be anything vapid about meal-times if, before a company of fellow-lovers met, each gave a moment to remembering words which surely do not apply only to prayer-meetings, "There am I in the midst"; and those other words too, "He was known of them in breaking of bread." Who that has known Him so, can ever be content with the merely ordinary?

It touches friendship. Friendship is a golden thing only if it be kept free from undisciplined attachment. We are not here to enjoy each other. We are here to do the will of God.

Are we of one mind about counting it an honour if in any measure we are made a spectacle unto the world, and to angels and to men?

If so, let us hearten one another on difficult days. Let each help the other to strengthen himself in God. "And David was greatly distressed; for the people spake of stoning him: but David strengthened himself in the Lord his God."

Are we of one mind in asking our Lord to mark His Cross upon our natural choices?

Then let us not be surprised when He does so.

> *And when the touch of death is here and there*
> *Laid on a thing most precious in our eyes,*
> *Let us not wonder, let us recognise*
> *The answer to this prayer.*

Are we of one mind in answering this question on the knees of our spirit, as many a man answered it in the days of old?

"Do you feel resolved generally to renounce without reserve

all those things which men in general love and embrace, and will you attempt and desire with all your strength what our Lord Jesus Christ loved and embraced? Do you consent to put on the livery of humiliation worn by Him, to suffer as He did, and for love of Him, contempt, calumnies and insults?"

Are we willing to be set at nought ?
If so, let us walk humbly with our God. Let none dream of an easy way to Jerusalem; there is no such way if our faces are set steadfastly to go there.

To read from some noble-minded book was often a bracing experience. It did not matter which facet of life that book touched; if it were gallant and true it had the effect of great marching music—we found ourselves thinking in the same rhythm. Or, as it seemed to me, such a book left us standing in a clean sea-wind; pettiness was blown away, for the penetrating words of such books shamed us into being ashamed of anything puerile.

But we always came back to the deepest we knew, and many a meeting of the Sisters of the Common Life closed with this prayer,

> *When the slothful flesh would murmur,*
> *Ease would cast her spell,*
> *Set our face as flint till twilight's*
> *Vesper bell.*

> *On Thy brow we see a thorn-crown,*
> *Blood-drops in Thy track,*
> *O forbid that we should ever*
> *Turn us back.*

There was a day when physical ills piled up, and the one who at that time was leading this Company felt the need of the simplest possible words of help. Lord, how live the life? how go on living it to the end ?

And the answer came in the simplest words that could be spoken : "Abide in Me, and I in you. As the branch cannot bear fruit of itself, except it abide in the vine; no more can ye, except ye abide in Me. I am the vine, Ye are the branches: He that abideth in Me, and I in him, the same bringeth forth much fruit: for without Me ye can do nothing. Continue ye in My love." Don't go away. It is like that other word, "Abide thou with me; with me thou shalt be in safeguard," which in Hebrew is, Sit down, settle down.

Settle down in My love and stay there. That is your part. The rest is Mine.

33. SEND US TO THE SEEKING HEART

We know Thee with us, Thou who art
Our Lord, our Unseen Guide.
O send us to the seeking heart,
The heart unsatified.

The sinful and the comfortless—
Great Healer, gather them
From out the careless crowd, to press
And touch Thy garment's hem.

MEANWHILE—that is, while Kohila and her fellow-nurses were preparing for the Place of Healing—they went out from time to time with their Sitties to the surrounding villages. A doctor or a nurse meets the most orthodox of Hindus and the most pugilistic of Muslims on neutral ground as it were—kindly human ground. But indeed anyone going out from this place where little children are known to be loved and cared for, and any friend met in that friendliest of places where the sick are tended, is fairly sure of a welcome, if only the visit be just a visit, and not too frequently repeated; for that would cause comment.

After a while we opened two Houses of Help, each with its dispensary and nurse, in towns about a day's journey north of Dohnavur, hoping for more freedom there than in the nearer villages. But the news of another who had confessed our Lord Jesus Christ had spread like wild-fire, and soon our workers found the old familiar taboo. People dare not face the suspicions, threats and curses that were sure to be the portion of any who went to those houses for help; and very little effective work could be done. Once again it was, Not peace but a sword.

So we had to wait for the fulfilment of our dream, Houses of Help in villages and towns. But Love is not baffled by baffling circumstances, and town and village came to us; prepared hearts were drawn by the call of Love. And we thanked God for those brought to us, for now they could listen quietly, unthreatened, unafraid. And often the great prayer of the medical missionary was manifestly answered: *Grant unto Thy servants to speak Thy word with all boldness, while Thou stretchest forth Thy hand to heal.*

Those days and these which lie about us now, follow familiar lines. The stripped, the wounded, the half-dead are with us always; and always there is the call on the compassion that sees and goes and binds up, "pouring in oil and wine."

Then, to anticipate a little, a Hall of Good Tidings was built where patients, their friends and others who came could be sure of a welcome. And Sunday evening lantern services were held on one of the wide verandahs of the Place of Healing. These meetings were so arranged that the picture-sheet which hung in the middle made a screen for the secluded women. They could sit in perfect privacy on one side and see and hear as well as the men on the other side of the sheet saw and heard. Such opportunities were new in this part of South India, and such hours were (and are) brimful of promise of blessing. "Take me out to sit in the wind," said an old Mohammedan gentleman one Sunday evening. He was not interested in the Gospel, and had not proposed "going o the meeting." But he took care that his chair was placed where that picture-sheet was visible and the voice of the preacher could be clearly heard. And the women who would fly to cover at the mere thought of being seen by any man not of their own family, felt as safe on their side of that sheet as if they were in their little rooms at home.

All this lay folded up in the heart of God like a bud waiting for the appointed moment to flower, when Kohila and her fellow-nurses crossed the bridge and walked round the growing-up buildings of the Place of Healing. And now to look back, as this book looks back over the two years of her Service in the Other Country, is like looking at something from which run golden lines in every direction. And we see the answer to the prayers of the years before, and understand what the Psalmist meant when he wrote, "Who can express the noble acts of the Lord or show forth all His praise?"

For it is not as though we were among the important of His servants or great in any way. Of the five ranks of His army, as Charles Fox used to call them, we belong to the fifth, "the things that are not."

But we have this great gain: we truly are one. " And when I go out preaching," said an Indian member of the Fellowship one morning, as he told of a succession of leadings after a few days absence from us, "I feel as if the whole family were with me, were at my back," and he waved a long, fine, pale-brown hand backwards over his shoulder. "It is a wonderful feeling, and things happen that would not happen if it were not so." It certainly is so. Those whose responsibility is the care of the children or the ill, and those who, like the angels, do essential things inconspicuously, are so one in spirit with the others who go out that they seem to be going out with them; and the joys and sorrows too are shared, for they belong to all. This naturally follows "the correspondence of convictions" that has been such a vital part of our life from the beginning; for it is true that "correspondence of personal convictions is the very foundation of spiritual fellowship. All that is not based on this corner-stone will fall; and if this stone crumble away, the fabric reared upon it will soon become a heap of ruins."

About the time Kohila went into training as a nurse, she came upon something in herself which we call briefly *Nãn thãn*. *Nãn* means I; *thãn* underlines the pronoun. Someone has said that there is nothing God will not do through one who does not care to whom the credit goes. *Nãn thãn* greatly cares. In Tamil, "deny thyself" is "renounce

thyself." Kohila set herself to renounce her *Nãn thãn*, so that she might
be free to serve others.

One of the prayers that we pray, as we think of the
Christless people who come to us and to whom we go, was set to
music by a friend who has done much for the prayer-music of the
Fellowship:

> *Love that never faileth,*
> *Love that all prevaileth,*
> *Saviour Christ, O hear me now*
> *And give Thy love to me.*

> *Round me souls are dying,*
> *Deep in darkness lying,*
> *Thou didst love them unto death,*
> *O give Thy love to me.*

The child of this story often sang those words, and as she
grew up into the love of God, her roots ran deep down into that love,
till she became one who could be counted upon to love. Among her
patients was the daughter of a rich landowner who has long resisted
the pleadings of the Spirit. He has come near the Kingdom more than
once, but has always drawn back just when hope had begun to dawn
for him. He would not allow his children to be taught, and he guarded
them most carefully from all Christian influences. But his daughter was
in sudden need of help, and he brought her here. Little could be said,
but she was loved, and told something of the love of God. And one
day she turned to Kohila, "Pray to your Saviour for me," she said, and
Kohila prayed. That daughter went back to her home where not one
word might be spoken about the Christ of God. She has followed her
little nurse into the great Unseen now; perhaps—who shall say that it is
not so? —that loving little nurse-evangelist is teaching her There all that
she was not allowed to teach her here. Perhaps such service is one of
the joys of the redeemed.

And perhaps another joy is theirs. Do they see from the heavenly side bright dreams come true? Even as this story is being written the Cloud which guides our tarryings and journeyings has moved forward, and lamps have been lighted in dark places.

34. FREE SOLITUDE

I have long thought it an error among all sorts that use not monastic lives, that they have no retreats for the afflicted, the tempted, the solitary, and the devout, where they might undisturbedly wait upon God, pass through their religious exercise, and, being thereby strengthened, may, with more power over their own spirits, enter into the business of the world again. *For divine pleasures are found in a free solitude.*

No Cross No Crown, William Penn (written in the Tower of London, 1668).

A STORY that tries to show the shaping of a worker here, must make room for the Forest. After the long walk up, the first joy is the Pool. One deep dive into that jade-coloured water, or a stiff fight up to the little waterfall (which if the river be full, pushes you back with all its might), or a rollicking hour with a dozen or more jubilant people, diving, swimming, splashing, shouting, washes off the tiredness of months of heat.

Merriment is the note of the Pool, and there is also an undertone of fortitude. Some of us have seen the tiny tree that grows in the cleft just above it, swept by raging floods. Every twig is stripped, but the roots hold fast; and those same twigs break out in green when the flood passes and the little tree can breathe again.

Then there is the joy of leisure for discovering our friends ("Friends are discovered, not made"). And it is good to have time enough to hear fully about things one had heard only in part. For the claims of the various worlds of nursery, schools, workshops, farm, Place of Healing and outposts, leave less time to be together than might be expected; and many things have to be left untold that all want to hear. But chiefly we need time with our God uninterrupted by clocks. Holidays may be mere waste of time, but they need not be.

173

So we bless God for our Free Solitude. When He allures us into the wilderness, He speaks comfortably to us; and when we go to the Potter's house, we receive new hope for the clay that was marred in the hands of the Potter. And we find a clearer vision in some secluded Valley of Vision; or waiting in the little ship that has nothing to do but wait on Him, we hear only the low voices of the water till He begins to speak.

These words are in tune with the Forest:
"As a statesman I often feel, beyond and beneath that ever-flowing stream of letters, interviews, deputations, committees, speeches and despatch-boxes, a still small voice that challenges all my efforts, searches out my motives, questions the meaning of everything that I do, and forces me to stand, as it were, in the full glare of the white light of eternity. And it is necessary for us that we should withdraw ourselves, if it be only for five minutes and ten minutes, that we may heed that voice and that we may think." *

The last year when we, who had loved Kohila from her curled-up kitten days, were to be together there, was when Abyssinia was ravished, and we shared in the grief of that land. So there was sorrow in the air that year. And yet a little memory that belongs to the life far above wars and griefs is folded up therein. To one of us, a melody had floated over the tree-tops, and she came into the Forest House in the bright morning, humming it softly. It seemed to ask for words to give body to its spirit, and when the words came, Kohila, in her shy little way, took possession of them and sang them over and over again.

That song was afterwards given to any who cared to have it, * but it was Kohila's first. And another she specially loved, so her fellow-

---

* *This Torch of Freedom*, Stanley Baldwin.   * No.83, *Toward Jerusalem*

nurse, Suseela, remembers, for she often heard her singing it as she
went about her work, was the song of the least lover:

> *I cannot bring Thee, O Beloved, ever,*
> *Pure song of woodland bird;*
> *And yet I know the song of Thy least lover*
> *In love is heard.*

Thanks be to Him who cares to hear the songs of His least
lovers.

She was still our "little Kohila," for she was among the
smallest in stature, but she was a fearless climber and adventured
far. One evening she and another girl went up the boundary path out
of sight or hearing of any of the houses; and they saw a bear.

We often see the spoor of bears by the path, and the stones
they have turned over in search of grubs; and several of us have
met the people of the Forest face to face. They have never disturbed
us, and we have never disturbed them, but a mother bear with a
cub near by is not likely to be friendly. (There was a bear on that
mountain-side which tore off the face of a man who quite
innocently appeared in her neighbourhood.) So, without stopping
to think, our two did the most foolish thing possible: they turned
and raced down the path. (They should, of course, have faded
into the forest, as the wise beasts do.) But what Kohila's companion
remembers best is this: "Never once while we ran, would Kohila
let me run behind; aways she was behind and I was in front. She
pushed me on, and kept behind herself. She was always like that."

It was a happy year, though shadowed sometimes by the
sorrows of others. Our Swiss sisters were with us, and the joy of
fellow-lovers from other lands was always fresh, like the fresh green
of the forest. Kohila was staying in the house built on the hillside
between the Jewel House (highest on the hill) and the Forest House

(lowest); the Jungle House we call it. But she used to come down in the evenings to learn the tune of the song she had made her own.

Then, every morning, there used to be the sound of merry voices as a party from the Jewel House or the Jungle House passed the Forest House on their way to the always delectable Pool.

The Annāchies who were in the Jewel House had an engaging way of looking in with a smile as they passed our windows, and of course the Junglers always ran in to say Good Morning. And on their way back, whichever happened to have been "pooling" would stop, and come in, and light up the little old brown house with their youth and joyfulness.

It was a happy time indeed, but it is not something past. It is ours for ever:

> *All that was ever ours is ours for ever.*
> *Glory of greenwood and the shining river,*
> *Joy of companionship of kindred mind,*
> *All, all is ours. It is not left behind*
> *Among the withered things that must decay,*
> *It is stored up for us,*
> *Somewhere, and for another day.*

And Kohila is ours for ever, too.

35. IN WHATSOEVER DAY

I love the people,
But do not like to stage me to their eyes.
Measure for Measure.

They (the three great Jewish prophets) all record how a vision of God was the essence of their call. Because they had seen God, and had heard His voice, they could, and therefore they must speak to their fellow-men.

Westcott.

FOR many years a meeting which no one would call easy to take has been held in the village church of Dohnavur—the women's meeting of the Harvest Festival.

Kohila had been going on with her God, and tasting afresh how gracious the Lord is. There was an hour when she had a new vision of His love, and this had led to something that all about her noticed: she was constantly drawing one and another aside that they might pray for someone in temptation or for a patient. In quiet, unobserved ways she had borne witness to Him for years, and many had been blessed by that witness; but she had not broken through and spoken at any public meeting, such as that Harvest Festival. She had a message to give, and yet could not pluck up courage to tell it out.

But there is a glorious word for all who are willing and yet feel quite unable: "They got not the land in possession by their own sword, neither did their own arm save them : but Thy right hand, and Thine arm, and the light of Thy countenance, because Thou hadst a favour unto them." Our little Kohila did earnestly desire to walk in the light of the ungrieved Countenance of the Lord, her Redeemer—but to speak to a large meeting? She could not face the thought of it.

177

And yet she had pondered the sequence of Ps.67:1, 2: "God be merciful unto us, and bless us; and cause His face to shine upon us; that Thy way may be known upon earth, Thy saving health among all nations." Tamil grammar reverses the order of the words : the reason for the prayer comes first. So that others may be illuminated (not so that we may bask in that light), we ask our God to cause His face to shine upon us.

At last there came a time when Kohila felt that she was called to witness to His Saving Health, and in that very meeting, that difficult meeting, the women's meeting at the Harvest Festival. She was willing to do anything rather than just this one thing. But she had been taught as Martin Luther said, "If I profess with the loudest voice and clearest exposition every portion of the truth of God except precisely that little point which the world and the devil are at that moment attacking, I am not confessing Christ, however boldly I may be professing Christ. Where the battle rages, there the loyalty of the soldier is proved, and to be steady on all the battle-field besides, is mere flight and disgrace if he flinches at that point." The world had nothing to do with the matter, for it knew nothing of it; but the devil knew. If Kohila flinched at that point, steadiness elsewhere would be mere flight and disgrace.

These festivals were initiated by Walker of Tinnevelly in the hope that they would be times of refreshment for the scattered Christians, and in some places they may be so. But they have for the most part degenerated into a huge rowdy fair, with as many meetings as possible crammed in because we are India, and India revels in meetings.

Imagine a church crowded with women in holiday mood. Many have babies, and babies rarely enjoy meetings, and say so in every tone of disapproval at their command. Imagine a great erection of palm-leaves on poles abutting upon the church. See the place packed to suffocation with a sticky mass of hot, very vocal village children. And hear, if you can, the two meetings going on at the same time; the women's on one side of the church door, the children's on the other. It was apparently impossible to carry on the children's meeting without perpetual and loud singing. Everything could be heard, of course, in the church ; and when the two streams of song met and clashed, I used to wonder what it sounded like in heaven. But, then, one might wonder about that all the time.

Soon, inevitably, some lucky youngster, tired of the meeting intended for his good, would slip off, and followed hopefully by any near enough the fringe of the crowd to escape, would climb the windows that looked into the church. Then, perching on the window-sills like so many young imps, they would shout news or encouragment to their mothers and aunts inside. An agitated catechist would immediately make a dive for those windows, and either bang them shut (which made it hotter than ever for us) or pull any dangling legs he could reach. Yells would follow; mothers and aunts would raise their voices in remonstrance, till a burst of singing from the other side of the door would drown everything except the buzz as of a million bees (for the stalls, of course, did not close down when meetings were going on), and the chattering of innumerable birds, which at that time built in the roof. To add to the confusion, there was the cackling of dozens of hens and crowing of cocks brought to be offered at the big meeting next day. They were cooped-up close by. And there was the protesting bleating of goats and kids tied up beside the church wall.

I do not know how the poor, moithered Pastors ever grappled with that women's meeting before 1900, when we came to Dohnavur. As soon as we did come, however, they shuffled it off their shoulders. It was our business henceforth. It seemed impossible to hope for spiritual results in the midst of such a racket, but just as the soldanella pushes up through deep snow, so does the Spirit of life work through apparently impossible conditions. (Snow, however, is not a good illustration. We would gladly have welcomed the cold quietness of snow.) The first year saw a notable conversion. The woman in whom the Spirit had His way was well known in her small world; she became a worker in another mission and was used to bring many to Christ. Once, when she came back to Dohnavur to see her old friends, and they fussed over her and she was tempted to pride, she stood up among them all, and quoted a deflating proverb, "However high I may fly, I am only a village sparrow."

Gradually things became more orderly, and as our children grew they helped, first by singing and then by speaking. Many a young girl took her first plunge into the frothy waters of publicity in that church and in that women's meeting, and it became our custom to ask for volunteers.

In the year 1936, when a younger worker was responsible for the meeting and asked for help, one of the first to offer was Kohila. Together, she and her Accal, Vineetha, had sat under the tamarind tree which is near our God's Garden, after the word had come to her that she could not mistake, but hardly knew how to obey. Under that tree there is a rough Cross of gneiss, the stone of which our mountains are made. By that Cross many a soul has entered into the experience of him who wrote, *The Lord will give strength unto His people; the Lord will bless His people with peace.* If we have strength and peace, we can go through anything.

The word that turned the delivering light of His countenance upon Kohila was our Lord's about confessing Him before men. To refuse this inward pressure would be to refuse to confess.

> *From subtle love of softening things,*
> *From easy choices, weakenings,*
> *From all that dims Thy Calvary,*
> *O Lamb of God, deliver me.*

The twelve who were to speak came to see me just before they went to the village church (twelve seems a large number, but some were to say only a few words). They all looked happy, some looked radiant; Kohila's face was more serious than radiant, but there was no hesitation there. When it came to her turn to speak, she stood beside the strong and gentle one who was leading. For a moment the words would not come. Then she looked to her Lord for courage. *In whatsoever day I shall call upon Thee, hear me speedily: Thou shalt abundantly provide me with Thy power in my soul* is the Septuagint rendering of Ps.138: 3. *In whatsoever day*— O Lord, that means to-day. "I felt at the conference that I had been given some power not always in me" —the words of one of our greatest (and humblest) soldiers might have been hers, simple little Indian nurse as she was, "Thou drewest near in the day that I called upon Thee : Thou saidst, Fear not."

And so it was that the upper and the nether springs were given. This victory of spirit over flesh had to be, if there was to be the unhindered breaking forth of the living water for the blessing of others, and be their work what it may, that is what we ask of our Caleb for our children.

This breaking forth of the waters from the springs followed on something that one of her friends had noticed. "I have often heard her singing most earnestly the prayer for a Passion for souls," one of them says. "It was her constant prayer."

> *Give me a passionate passion for souls,*
> *Give me a pity that yearns;*
> *Give me the love that loves unto death,*
> *Give me the fire that burns;*
> *Give me, O Lord, to be fervent in prayer,*
> *Pouring out all for the lost;*
> *Give me to pray in the Conqueror's Name,*
> *Spirit of Pentecost.*

A prayer for the spirit of burning added later, ends with words that she also sang :

Lord, we believe, we accept, we adore,
Less than the least though we be,
Fire of Love, burn in us, burn evermore,
Till we burn out for Thee.

But burning out for God does not mean anything that looks great. The tender old Jewish story about Moses and the lost lamb tells part of what it means. Moses was shepherding Jethro's flock, the story says, when a lamb wandered away. He followed it and found it drinking at a brook. "Had I known that thou wast thirsty," he said to the little lamb, "I would have taken thee in my arms and carried thee hither." And a heavenly Voice spoke: "Thou art fit to shepherd Israel."

36. GOD NEVER WASTES HIS SERVANTS' TIME

(My) days were fashioned (already) when (as yet) there was none among them. Ps. 139. 16. From *The Book of the Psalms,* in the Parchment Library.

It sounds a simple thing to go and fetch a baby when some kind friend has been working for its salvation and wires to us to come for it. But we know what it is to be disappointed, for anything may happen at the last moment. The child whom we exist to save is never "unwanted."

Some two hundred miles distant from Dohnavur is a town, famous in Indian history, whose temple is one of the sights of the South. If the hand of Amalek had had its way, many a child now safe with us would have been absorbed into the life of that temple. But that hand has dared too much; and so, like Moses, we build our altar and call the name of it Jehovah Nissi, the Lord our Banner. *Because the hand of Amalek is against the throne of the Lord, therefore the Lord will have war with Amalek from generation to generation.*

One day, in the stifling month of September, a wire came from that temple-town asking us to send for a baby-boy who had been saved there. We sent Kohila with an old grannie as escort, their directions were to wait in an appointed place till the baby was brought.

But they arrived in the late evening, tired and confused after those many hours in the crowded train, and Kohila had fever. By some mistake they missed the baby, and next day, distressed and perplexed, they contrived to lose themselves in the bazaar on their way to the station.

And then, the usual—the blessed usual—happened; Goodness and Mercy had followed them. Out of the 120,000 of that town, suddenly one appeared—a car-driver who had been in Dohnavur years ago for a short time. He recognised the Dohnavur colours and stopped his car.

"I have a fare," he said, "but wait here for half an hour, and I will come for you." And he came in half an hour and took our two tired people to the station. By only a minute or two they caught their train home.

Next day about noon they arrived, grateful for the goodness and mercy that had followed them, but weary and disappointed, for they felt that they had wasted time and the journey-money too. But God never wastes His servants' time or their money. During the few hours Kohila had spent in that town she had made friends with one whose heart was ready to be touched about the children in danger. "I will search, and by the grace of God I will find," she said, "and I will come to Dohnavur bringing a little child."

And that promise was kept. A few weeks later—but by that time Kohila had passed on to what the children think of as a beautiful Upstairs-Nursery—that woman arrived at Dohnavur, and in her arms was a little child.

"Where is that meritorious one?" she asked. "She promised me a welcome." And when she had heard that her minutes had hastened to their end, "She will welcome me There," she said, content.

Meanwhile, the boy Kohila had gone to fetch had been kept safely; and the next one who went for him did not return empty-handed.

In ways like this our Father often comes near to us and tells us that our times are in His hand. Our days are fashioned already ; O great Fashioner of our days, Thou hast fashioned my to-day.

37. THE WHEEL

I am no longer my own, but Thine. Put me to what Thou wilt, rank me with whom Thou wilt; put me to doing, put me to suffering; let me be employed for Thee or laid aside for Thee, exalted for Thee or brought low for Thee; let me be full, let me be empty; let me have all things, let me have nothing; I freely and heartily yield all things to Thy pleasure and disposal.

From the Covenant Service of the Methodist Church.

IN the House of Prayer is a wheel of teak-wood, eleven feet seven inches in circumference—an ordinary old cartwheel scraped and polished. It is set on a stand, and so adjusted that it can be turned. The rim is made of six segments fitted onto twelve spokes. On each segment is written in Tamil a word which indicates some part of the Fellowship work. The whole is bound by a band of shining brass which looks like gold, and signifies the bond of love which holds us together. The wheel stands in the House of Prayer, so that we may be constantly reminded of our high calling, and helped to magnify our office and do the will of God from the heart.

This wheel was the illustration used at one of the two last special meetings which Kohila attended. Our Annāchie, Peace of God, had thought out the illustration. He took that meeting.

Now, as this book is nearing its end, his brother has chanced (as we say) to gather into a few sentences for the family's help the thought that underlies the writing from first page to last. "He put us all into those sentences," said one of the younger workers in telling me of it. "It was as if he were giving us each a message, not one of us was forgotten. It was like the Wheel. We all found ourselves there."

This is the sum of that message :
There they dwelt with the King for His work.

185

What is your work? Whatever it be, the Lord, the King, has done that kind of work Himself, and you dwell with Him here for His work.

Is your work with the little children, carrying them about, loving them?

In His love and in His pity He redeemed them; and He bare them, and carried them all the days of old. Thou hast seen how that the Lord thy God bare thee, as a man doth bear his son, in all the way that ye went.

He has done the work that you are doing. You dwell with Him here for His work.

Is your work teaching the children to walk, giving them their food?

God says, When Israel was a child, then I loved him, And I it was that taught Ephraim to walk, —He took them upon His arms. I drew them with bands of a man, with cords of love; I gently caused them to eat.*

Is your work to " mother," comfort and strengthen? †

As one whom his mother comforteth, so will I comfort you, saith the Lord. The word comfort is from two Latin words meaning " with " and " strong " —He is with us to make us strong. Comfort is not soft, weakening commiseration; it is true, strengthening love.

Is your work the disciplining of younger brothers and sisters, patiently and lovingly leading them on, holding them unfalteringly to God's highest?

---

* Hosea 11: 1, 3, 4, Darby. Cords of love—the leading-strings used to guide a little child who is learning to walk. Then the picture changes; we see a man caring for his bullock, lifting the yoke and gently pushing his food to him. Keil and Delitzsch.

† I Thess. 2: 7, Weymouth. Gentle as a mother is when she tenderly nurses her own children.

What son is there whom his Father does not discipline? He does it for our certain good in order that we may become sharers in His own holy character.*

Is your work in the sewing-room?
Unto Adam also and to his wife did the Lord God make coats of skin, and clothed them.

He has done the work that you are doing. You dwell here with the King for His work.

Is your work cooking, lighting fires in the kitchen in the early morning, getting food ready for others?
When the morning was now come, Jesus stood on the shore; but the disciples knew not that it was Jesus. As soon then as they were come to land, they saw a fire of coals there, and fish laid thereon, and bread. Jesus saith unto them, Come this way and have breakfast. †

He has done the work that you are doing. You dwell here with the King for His work.

Is your work tending people, washing patients?
Jesus riseth from supper, and laid aside His garments; and took a towel, and girded Himself. After that He poureth water into a basin, and began to wash the disciples' feet, and to wipe them with the towel where with He was girded.

He has done the work that you are doing. You dwell here with the King for His work.

Is your work nursing, bandaging sores?
He healeth the broken in heart, and bindeth up their wounds

---

* Heb. 12:10, Weymouth   † John 21:12, Weymouth.

He has done the work that you are doing. You dwell here with the King for His work.

Is your work cleaning?
I will cleanse them from all their iniquity—that is harder work than cleaning floors or washing clothes.

Is your work writing—writing on a blackboard in school, writing in the office, answering letters?
He declared unto you His covenant, which He commanded you to perform, even ten commandments; and He wrote them upon two tables of stone. The Lord shall count when He writeth up the people, that this man was born there. God says, I have written to him the great things of My law. Jesus stooped down and wrote on the ground. They are written in the Lamb's book of life.

He has done the work that you are doing. You dwell here with the King for His work.

Is your work account-keeping, teaching or learning arithmetic, or the names of things hard to remember?
He telleth the number of the stars; He calleth them all by their names. Even the very hairs of your head are all numbered.

He has done the work that you are doing. You dwell here with the King for His work.

Is your work in the farm with the animals?
He shall feed His flock like a shepherd: He shall gather the lambs with His arm, and carry them in His bosom.
Is your work in the engine-room, or the carpentering shops? Is it making things or mending things?
O give thanks unto the Lord that made great lights.

Through faith we understand that the worlds were framed by the word of God. (The verb is the same as that used in Matt. 4: 21, *mending* their nets.) Is not this the Carpenter? and they were offended at Him.

He has done the work that you are doing. You dwell here with the King for His work.

Is your work praying for others, enduring temptation, suffering for His sake?

He steadfastly set His face to go to Jerusalem. Jesus kneeled down and prayed. And, being in an agony, He prayed more earnestly: and His sweat was as it were great drops of blood falling down to the ground.

Surely He hath borne our griefs, and carried our sorrows. He, for the joy that was set before Him, endured the Cross.

He has done the work that you are doing. You dwe l here with the King of His work.

Is your work to take the Gospel to those who need it, but do not know their need?

Your King did that work: I have spread out My hands all the day unto a rebellious people, which walketh in a way that was not good, after their own thoughts. In the last day, that great day of the feast, Jesus stood and cried, saying, If any man thirst, let him come unto Me and drink. But our Lord did more than speak, He went about *doing* good. Dwell thus with the King for His work.

38. THE FIRST BAPTISM IN THE HALL OF GOOD TIDINGS

For the quiet joy of duty,
Praise, praise I sing;
  For the commonplace and lowly,
  Set with pleasure high and holy,
  In each unromantic thing,
  Praise, praise to Thee, my King.

For the solemn joy of battle,
Praise, praise I sing;
  For the wounds and sore distresses,
  For the love that soothes and blesses,
  Strength in weakness perfecting,
  Praise, praise to Thee, my King.

For the splendid joy of triumph,
Praise, praise I sing;
  For the joy all joys excelling,
  Passing, passing human telling,
  Joy to see Thee conquering,
  Praise, praise to Thee, my King.

ONE more short chapter shall look beyond what Kohila saw, unless, indeed, she saw it through clearer air than ours. It was a day following closely upon the other which drew the common things of the Wheel into the light and the companionship of God.

It was the day of the first baptism in the Hall of Good Tidings. Some time ago, in a hospital in another country, a helpless, suffering man was by accident dropped as his stretcher-bearers carried him; and his leg was badly broken. With the courage of despair, he determined to return to Southern India, where his home was.

Without even a splint on that injured limb, in pain that cannot be described, he travelled by boat and bus till at last he came to his

191

house near Joyous City, a little town of about five thousand, a few miles from Dohnavur.

Soon afterwards he was brought to the Place of Healing, a wreck, far too wretched to think of anything but his pain.

But gradually, as it passed, his heart began to open to the love all round him, and so at last to the Love of all loves, and he returned home believing in our Lord Jesus Christ and openly confessing Him.

Among the outflowings from the Place of Healing is village-work, and soon young nursing-brothers (our boys in training in the Place of Healing) went to see him. They found him so very ill again that he was quite unable to do anything for himself; and because of his confession of Christ as his Lord and Saviour, he was untended by his family. He would soon have died for lack of care and food.

It was impossible to leave him like that, so he was brought back to the Place of Spiritual Healing, and after being nourished and strengthened, he went on learning and reading and witnessing. Everyone spoke of him in the same way: radiance—not just ordinary decorous happiness, but *radiance* was the word they used as they spoke of him.

After a while he had several operations; and the chimes, rung in the Room of Vision above the theatre and in our House of Prayer, called us all to pray. This help relieved the worst conditions, but tubercular trouble complicated his case. And yet there he lay, radiant and eager to share his illuminating treasure with all who would listen. "Come, do listen to this word which I have just read," he would say as someone passed him, "Is it not comforting? And it is true. True indeed I have proved it to be. Not mere words are these words of the Book. They are gold."

Then the day came when he felt he must witness to his faith by baptism, and as he could not possibly go to Mountain-foot-Water, where our baptisms are usually held, he was carried to the Hall.

One who was there described that half-hour, and the shining of her eyes as she talked showed it even more clearly than her words: "It was wonderful. It was like being at the Pool of Bethesda. There were many people—two hundred or more—sick and well, all sorts of people. You would see one who was tired make a sign, and instantly Annāchie saw it, and the sick one was gently carried away. Women and children came in and out, but so quietly that there was no disturbance. You never noticed them.

"When the four Purples (our nursing-brothers who wear purple) carried the stretcher in, they went up to the front, and stood there; and Annāchie and the Pastor stood there too." ("They and Murray in the centre at the back, holding the water, made a lovely group, and the fatherly old Pastor completed the picture," writes another who was there.) "It was wonderful to hear the ringing answers to the Pastor's questions: everyone could hear them. And the little children sang, *Be thou faithful unto death, and I will give thee a crown of life,* just as they sing at our baptisms by Mountain-foot-Water. It was all so joyful and free and quiet and simple; a beautiful hour."

It was hours like this that our girls and boys, inspired by loving leaders, saw by faith as they prepared for service in the Place round which years of thought had gathered. And Kohila was very happy as she and her companions went up to the Forest two months before that Place of many prayers was opened.

39. LILIES

What will it be, when like the wind-blown spray
Our spirits rise and fly away, away?

O lighter than the silvery, airy foam
We shall float free. All winds will blow us home.

We shall forget the garments that we wore:
We shall not need them ever any more.

We shall put on our immortality,
And we shall see Thy face and be like Thee,

And serve Thee, Lord, who hast so much forgiven,
Serve Thee in holiness—and this is heaven.

"I ACCEPT; I approve; I give thanks" —these words belong to one of the last birthday meetings when we were all together, and had been thinking of that good and lovable (as the Tamil has it) and perfect will of God. The words sum up our thoughts as we look back upon that holiday.

"She was like a little star of love," wrote one of her sisters, speaking of the few days spent together before she passed on. It is good to think that the word Lady Harcourt wrote to her father about Abraham Lincoln, "I echo your 'thank God' that we always appreciated him before he was taken from us," was true in our case about our little nurse. We miss something when we are blind to the life and the character of a companion till he or she has gone. "One day we were going up the river and someone was tired and began to speak a little unhappily," the letter continues, "but in a moment Kohila was beside her, and she was happy again. And we sang and sang." To sing merrily unto God our Strength seems natural in the singing woods, and by the singing waters.

There is another word that always recalls Kohila. It is that beautiful little Psalm which closes the Septuagint Book of Psalms; the heading says it is David's: "I was small among my brethren, and youngest in my father's house: I tended my father's sheep. My hands formed a musical instrument, and my fingers tuned a psaltery. And who shall tell my Lord? the Lord Himself, He Himself hears." Little Kohila, smallest among her sisters, might have said with King David, "And who shall tell my Lord? Who need tell Him? The Lord Himself, He Himself hears."

Almost every evening brings some pleasure to those who are carrying on in Dohnavur during the hot weather. Ferns and hill-flowers come, and lovely crimson leaves, and above all the dearest of letters from our children and others who are in the Forest. The green things are packed in tins, and are always cool and fresh and smelling of the woods. The letters, sometimes illustrated with comical drawings, show us life as it is up there, with its family jokes and adventures.

There was once one of a frieze of girls standing on the beams that run under the roof of the Jewel-House porch. The long line of blue, lilac, purple and crimson-draped figures have a sort of Grecian air. On the steps are the Sitties, one with an electric torch searching the groundfloor; for, of course, no one thought of looking up to the roof for the missing girls. And another showed a small girl scrambling among rocks, followed by an enormous python, whose open mouth has all but seized her agitated pigtail.

Among the last letters Kohila wrote was one to her Sittie whose name means Aid. She wrote in Tamil. This is a translation:

"I have not enough words to praise Him who has given me this time up here. I understand now that there are no words to express the beauty and glory of the works of His hands.

"When I see how His creatures never grieve Him, but keep on praising Him all the time, I am astonished. I, His child, have often been disobedient to His dear Will. I am very sad when I think of that. Please pray for me that I may receive fully in Him all the blessings that He is wanting to give me.

"Pray that I may use the time that He has lovingly given here to think of the souls of others and pray for them faithfully in Him."

Then came something that went deeper, though it may read simply : Kohila proposed sharing her room (the new little room which had been hers after she gave up her old room) with a younger nurse who often needed a helping hand.

It was the dearest thing she had to give—her privacy. And when I heard of how she had stripped it off for love of Him who did that very thing long ago for love of us, I was reminded of a family of medical missionaries in Southern India. For many years, until a Nursing Home was built near by, they went on doing this inconspicuous, kindly thing as a matter of course. Not only their patients, but their patients' relations, were welcomed to that house, and husband and wife seldom knew what it was to have a meal alone. They made nothing of it. They will hardly recognise themselves if they ever read this story, but that was the life they lived, and our little Kohila was following a greater tradition than she knew when she wrote, "Let R. share my room."

And then came a morning when, eager to gather quantities of a purple flower for a fellow-nurse's Coming-day, Kohila went far up the mountains with two others, and climbing a rock too steep for her, but which her ardent heart had not thought of as too steep, she slipped and fell. And then,

> *"Carried by angels" —it is all we know*
> *Of how they go;*
> *We heard it long ago,*
> *It is enough; they are not lonely there.*
> *Lost nestlings blown about in fields of air.*
> *The angels carry them; the way, they know.*
> *Our kind Lord told us so.*

Then the rain came down in sheets, but the Annãchies who were such strong brothers to the distressed company that day, the Sitties, of whom one, to our relief, was the doctor, Christian Rogan, who suffered with their Indian sisters in the shock and grief, and Kohila's closest friends, do not, as they look back, remember the pouring rain that turned the mountains black, and made the forest one dark night as they carried her down the mountain-side to the house she had left, blithe as a bird, a few hours before. They remember a lovingkindness that shone through everything; the flowers which their Annãchie brought down to us to lighten the day when she was laid to rest in God's Garden; the light, the inextinguishable light, that turned the very darkness into light even then for us all—that is what they remember.

It was the old truth in a new form. Never, never can the darkness overcome the light; always it is the light that overcomes the darkness. All the foundations of the earth are out of course. Even so, they shall know, those who darken the air from age to age, they shall know that Thou, whose name alone is Jehovah, art the most high over all the earth. Light must win in any contest—in the end.

A year later, on the anniversary of her Celestial birthday, a little company of those who were in the Forest then, met at Kohila's Rock to offer worship and praise to Him whose name is holy.

It was a perfect evening, and the forest world and the mountain world and those who were gathered in that upper air were of one accord. In His temple that evening everything said, Glory. Among the

many letters that told us of that hour spent between heaven and
earth was one from Kohila's sister, Tara. "As we were going up
through the woods down which she was carried that day a year ago,
I felt afraid. But when we reached the rock, we saw that the whole
place was a garden of flowers—balsams, and the purple flowers she
had climbed to reach, and pink and mauve orchids; and in the deep
crevice running down the rock and everywhere about it, there were
white lilies. It was as if the angels had planted them there on purpose
to give us joy that day. And all my fear fled. It flew away.

"Then, sitting on a flat place on the rock, we sang some of
our own songs, 'O God of stars and flowers, forgive our blindness,'
'O Splendour of God's Will,' and the one about the lilies among
the high mountains. Then Murray Annãchie led us in worship, reading
very glorious verses, and after a Silence he gave thanks for Kohila."

This was the thanksgiving :

Blessed and holy, O Lord, art Thou, who art the
Resurrection and the life. For Thy Presence in this holy place,

We thank Thee.

For Kohila, for her faithfulness, for her love of little
children, for her care for all who suffered,

We thank Thee.

For her joy as she sees Thy face, and serves Thee in the
Company of the Redeemed,

We thank Thee.

For all who stand before the Throne and before the Lamb
saying, Worthy is the Lamb that was slain to receive power, and

riches, and wisdom, and strength and honour and glory,

> *We thank Thee.*
> Lift up your hearts.
> *We lift them up unto the Lord.*
> Heaven and earth are full of Thy glory.
> *Glory be to Thee, O Lord, most high.*

Then there was Silence again, and then the prayer which so often ends our prayers,

> Teach us good Lord,
> To serve Thee more faithfully;
> To give and not to count the cost;
> To fight and not to heed the wounds;
> To toil and not to seek for rest;
> To labour and not to ask for any reward,
> Save that of knowing that we do Thy will,
> O Lord, our God. Amen.

And then they stood for a while in the after-glow, hushed by the sense of awe that comes down upon the spirit like a cloud, moving gently over it, brooding upon it. Everything, even the summits above them, the forest, the rocks, and the flowers that caught the golden light on their delicate faces, all seemed less real at that moment than the unseen Presences about them. And everything seemed small; but as one wrote, "We ourselves were the smallest things of all. Soon we had to hasten home, and we went slipping and slithering down through the steep forest till we came to the riverbed. It was good to feel rock underfoot once more, and I couldn't help thanking God for the Rock that He always gives us for our feet. I should hate to walk on loose earth and leaves when the Rock is there."

Then, calmed by the sweet influences of that upper world, comforted by song and by the great Words of Scripture, and strengthened by prayer, Tara ends her letter very peacefully, "Until then I had been afraid to look toward that hillside, but now it reminds me of Him and His majesty, and no more of earthly fears. When I slept last night I dreamt of that place of flowers, and of nothing else. And whenever I woke I could smell the lilies which were just outside the door."

And so our story of the shaping of a nurse ends in a place of flowers. If it had not been for some who will perhaps read this tale, and whose hearts were touched about these children of India, it might have been very different. Behind the life of this happy child, happy girl, happy warrior, lay no fair garden, nothing holy, nothing beautiful; but only the shadow of temple walls. Could anything be too much to do or to suffer, if only we may save such as she from what that shadow means?

"She passed from one garden to another," wrote a young Annãchie who had marvelled at the beauty of the place; and an older Sittie wrote of a boy drawn also from the Land of Shadows,—"he came over the brow of the hill in the after-glow, and his arms were full of pure white lilies."

DOHNAVUR FELLOWSHIP BOOKS

BY Amy Carmichael
  Candles in the Dark (selected letters)
  Edges of His Ways (daily readings)
  Figures of the True (illustrated)
*Fragments that Remain
*God's Missionary
  Gold by Moonlight (illustrated)
  Gold Cord - The Story of a Fellowship
  His Thoughts Said
  If
  Mimosa (the joys & struggles of a child who believed
  Mountain Breezes (poetry)
  Rose from Brier (from the ill to the ill)
  Thou givest . . . They Gather (selected writings)
*Toward Jerusalem (poetry)
  Whispers of His Power (daily readings)

By other authors
  Amy Carmichael of Dohavur
          by Bishop Frank Houghton
  A Chance to Die (biography of Amy Carmichael)
          by Elisabeth Elliot
  Learning of God (Anthology of A.C.'s writings
          by Stuart & Brenda Blanche)
*The Timothys - Indian Schoolgirls
          by B Trehane
*At BBC Corner I Remember Amy Carmichael
          by Margaret Wilkinson
*Patients & Patience
          by Nancy Robbins
* From the Dohnavur office and UK office only

Copies of the "**Dohnavur Fellowship Books**," and all other information can be obtained from:

> **The Dohnavur Fellowship**
> Dohnavur
> Tirunelveli Dt. 627 102
> Tamil Nadu
> India   - **Sales within India only -**

or from

> The Secretary
> **The Dohnavur Fellowship Corpn.**
> 15, Elm Drive
> Harrow
> Middx. HA2 7BS
> England, UK

or from Christian bookshops in the UK and elsewhere.

The majority of the books are also available in the USA by Mail Order from the publisher :-

> **The Christian Literature Crusade Book Centre**
> P.O Box 1449
> Fort Washington, PA 19034, USA

several of the books in English Braille can be obtained on loan from:

> **The National Library for the Blind**
> 35 Great Smith Street
> London SWI, UK

or from

> **The Braille Circulating Library**
> 203 North Jefferson Street
> Richmond
> Virginia, USA